THAI STORIES
FOR LANGUAGE LEARNERS

THAI STORIES
FOR LANGUAGE LEARNERS

Jintana Rattanakhemakorn & Dylan Southard
Illustrated by Patcharee Meesukhon

TUTTLE Publishing
Tokyo | Rutland, Vermont | Singapore

Contents

Introduction

Short stories are a great way for you to learn a language! This book is specifically designed for learners of the Thai language who wish to practice reading at the beginning to intermediate levels and higher. Here you will find twenty-eight stories of different lengths and at different levels of language complexity on a variety of topics. The accompanying audio recordings in English and Thai also help you to deepen your comprehension of the stories and improve your pronunciation and feel for the language.

These stories are all well-known Thai fables and folktales which have been passed down from one generation to the next for centuries. The shorter stories are adapted Thai versions of universal Aesop-type fables. The longer stories are modified versions of traditional folktales with roots in the Thai oral tradition, classical Thai literature, and the Indian Jataka Tales (which describe the past lives of the Buddha). The original Thai versions were first composed in poetry by kings and poets during the Ayutthaya period (in the beginning of the 17th century) and the early Rattanakosin period (in the 18th century).

Most of these stories contain moral lessons promoting honesty, and some are tales of spirits and supernatural beings involving Thai kings and queens, with giants and divine heroes and heroines. They are drawn from Thai children's books and textbooks used in primary school. Each story has been selected based on the complexity of the vocabulary, sentence structure and plot lines. The chosen stories have been rewritten and simplified to be suitable for non-native speakers at various levels. Hence, this book can be used by learners who are just beginning to read and write the language and would like additional practice, as well as for general readers interested in learning about Thai culture.

Each story is presented in parallel English and Thai on facing pages. A list of key vocabulary for each story is also provided in Thai script and Romanized Thai along with the English meaning, followed by a set of questions and writing activities. At the end of the book, you will find a Thai pronunciation guide where the consonants, vowels and tones are introduced. After that, you can practice writing vowels and consonants before moving on to reading and writing Thai syllables, words and sentences. You should also practice reading the stories aloud while listening to the accompanying audio recording in order to gain a better understanding of the stories and improve your pronunciation. It is very helpful to memorize a few of the stories completely using the recordings. This will help you develop a good feel for the language!

This book has everything you need to not only help you to improve your reading skills and expand your vocabulary. You will also learn about Thai beliefs and customs and how people in Thailand live their daily lives and think about their morals and their goals.

—Jintana Rattanakhemakorn & Dylan Southard

The Piglet and the Goat

Once there was a fat piglet who had hidden among a herd of goats. When the goatherd discovered the piglet, he chased after her and tried to catch her. The piglet squealed loudly, "Oink! Oink!" and scurried quickly away, where she was once again corralled into the same pen as the goats.

One day, a farmer came in and snatched up the piglet, but again she squealed noisily and struggled for dear life.

The goats saw this and were disgusted with the piglet for crying out so loudly. The two of them grumbled about the racket she was causing, saying, "We have been caught time and time again but have never cried so noisily as that piglet does after being caught only once."

The piglet heard this and replied, "Being caught is different for you than it is for me. He only catches you to milk you. But he chases after me to cut me up. He wants to take my life!" The piglet shouted this back as she ran for her life.

ลูกหมูกับแพะ

ลูกหมูอ้วนตัวหนึ่งแอบหลบหนีเข้าไปหลบอยู่ในฝูงแพะเมื่อคนเลี้ยงแพะ
มาพบเข้าก็วิ่งไล่จับมัน เจ้าลูกหมูส่งเสียงร้อง "อู๊ด อู๊ด" ดังลั่น และวิ่ง
หนีอุตลุด ลูกหมูถูกจับขังรวมกับแพะไว้ในคอกเดียวกัน

วันหนึ่งชาวนาเข้ามาจับลูกหมู แต่มันกลับร้องโวยวายและดิ้นหนีอย่าง
สุดชีวิต

แพะเห็นเข้าเกิดความหมั่นไส้ลูกหมูที่ร้องเสียงดัง แพะสองตัวจึงบ่น
กับเรื่องเสียงร้องของเจ้าลูกหมูว่า "พวกเราถูกจับบ่อย ๆ แต่ก็ไม่เคยส่ง
เสียงร้องอย่างเจ้าซึ่งโดนจับเพียงครั้งแรก"

ลูกหมูได้ฟังจึงตอบว่า "การจับระหว่างเจ้ากับข้ามันต่างกัน เขาจับพวก
เจ้าไปเพื่อรีดนมเท่านั้น แต่เขาจะจับข้าไปเชือดต่างหากล่ะ เขาต้องการ
ชีวิตของข้า" ลูกหมูตะโกนตอบพร้อมวิ่งหนีสุดชีวิต

Vocabulary

1	แอบ/หลบ	àehp/lòp	to hide
2	คนเลี้ยงแพะ	khon líang pháe	goatherd
3	หนี	nǐi	to scurry/run away
4	ฝูง	fǔung	herd
5	ไล่	lâi	to chase after
6	จับ	jàp	to catch
7	ขัง	khǎng	to corral, cage
8	อุตลุด	ùt tà lùt	quickly
9	คอก	khâwk	pen (for confining animals)
10	ร้องโวยวาย	ráwng wohy waay	to cry out (squeal) noisily
11	สุดชีวิต	sùt chii wít	for dear life
12	หมั่นไส้	màn sâi	to be disgusted
13	รีดนม	rîit nom	to (draw) milk
14	เชือด	chûeat	to slaughter/kill
15	ตะโกน	tà gohn	to shout

Comprehension Questions

1. Where was the piglet corralled?

2. Who discovered the piglet and tried to catch it?

3. What would happen to the piglet if it were caught?

Writing Activity

Write briefly about how you feel about the piglet.

The Rooster and the Jewel

One morning, a rooster was scratching at the ground in a rice field, looking for grains of rice. As he was clawing at the soil, he saw something glittering beneath it. He scraped off the dirt and there, in front of him, was a sparkling jewel. He pecked at the jewel and tried to eat it, but it was hard and too big to swallow. He could only stare at it and say, "Beautiful jewel, you are useless. A grain of rice would be of more use." Having said this, the rooster flung the jewel far away—having lost all interest in it—and continued looking for grains of rice.

Vocabulary

1	คุ้ยเขี่ย	**khúy khìa**	to scratch
2	เมล็ดข้าว	**má-lét khâaw**	grain of rice
3	ดิน	**din**	soil
4	พบ/เจอ	**phóp/jerr**	to see
5	พลอย	**phlawy**	jewel
6	สะท้อนแสง/แวววาว	**sà tháwn săehng/waehw waaw**	sparkling
7	ข้างหน้า	**khâang nâa**	in front of
8	จิก	**jìk**	to peck
9	แข็ง	**khăeng**	hard
10	มอง	**mawng**	to stare
11	ไม่มีประโยชน์	**mâi mii prà-yòht**	useless
12	เขวี้ยง	**khwîang**	to fling
13	ไม่สนใจ	**mâi sŏn jai**	to lose interest

ไก่ได้พลอย

ยามเช้าของวันหนึ่งมีไก่ตัวหนึ่งกำลังคุ้ยเขี่ยหาเมล็ดข้าวตามพื้นดินอยู่
กลางทุ่งนา ระหว่างที่คุ้ยดินอยู่นั้น มันเห็นก้อนวาววับอยู่ภายใต้กองดิน
นั้นเอง เจ้าไก่จึงคุ้ยเขี่ยดินออกจนพบเม็ดพลอยเม็ดหนึ่งสะท้อนแสง
แวววาวอยู่ข้างหน้า เจ้าไก่จิกเม็ดพลอยขึ้นมาและพยายามที่จะกิน แต่เม็ด
พลอยก้อนนั้นกลับแข็งและใหญ่กว่าที่จะกินลงไปในท้องได้ จึงได้แต่ยืน
มองพลอยเม็ดนั้นแล้วพูดว่า "พลอยแสนสวย เจ้าไม่มีประโยชน์อะไรเลย
หากฉันเจอข้าวเปลือกสักเม็ด คงจะมีประโยชน์กว่า" พูดจบเจ้าไก่ก็เขวี้ยง
เม็ดพลอยเม็ดนั้นไปไกลจากตัว แล้วจึงจิกหาเม็ดข้าวที่ตกอยู่ต่อไป โดยไม่
สนใจพลอยเม็ดนั้นเลย

Comprehension Questions

1. What was the rooster looking for on the ground?
2. Where did the rooster find the jewel?
3. What did the rooster do when he saw the jewel?
4. Why was he not happy with finding the jewel?

Writing Activity

What would you do if you found a jewel?

The Cat and the Mice

There was once a house that was infested with scores of mice, so the owner took in a cat to get rid of them. The cat soon noticed that the house was completely overrun with mice, but she caught them every day, one by one, and their number slowly decreased. The remaining mice were worried for their safety, so they all agreed that they would no longer come into the kitchen to look for food. They would only go out in search of food near their holes, into which they could quickly escape when the cat approached.

Soon the cat who was prowling the kitchen did not see a single mouse, and she started to wonder why the mice were not coming out to look for food as before. So, she hatched a plan to trick them into coming out. She lay on the floor unmoving, in order to fool the mice into thinking she had died. But there was one mouse who realized immediately that the cat was only playing dead. Slowly, he tiptoed out of the hole and said to the cat, "Cunning cat, we know well that this is a ruse. My friends and I aren't fooled by your little trick at all!" Having said this, he scurried back into his hole.

แมวกับหนู

บ้านหลังหนึ่งมีหนูชุกชุมมาก เจ้าของบ้านจึงนำแมวมาเลี้ยงไว้เพื่อกำจัด
หนู วันหนึ่งแมวเริ่มสังเกตเห็นว่ามีหนูอยู่ในบ้านเต็มไปหมด จึงคอยจับ
หนูกินทีละตัว ๆ ทุกวันจนกระทั่งหนูค่อย ๆ ลดจำนวนลง พวกหนูที่
เหลือรู้สึกเป็นห่วงความปลอดภัยของตัวเอง จึงตกลงกันว่าจะหาอาหาร
บริเวณที่ใกล้กับรูเท่านั้นเพื่อที่จะหลบเข้ารูได้ทันเมื่อแมวเข้ามาใกล้ และ
จะไม่ลงไปกินอาหารที่ห้องครัวอีกเป็นอันขาด

หลังจากนั้นแมวที่เฝ้าอยู่ตรงห้องครัวก็ไม่เห็นหนูอีกเลยแม้แต่ตัว
เดียว ทำให้แมวเริ่มสงสัยว่าทำไมพวกหนูจึงไม่ออกมาหาอาหารเหมือน
เช่นเคย จึงคิดแผนการหลอกล่อให้หนูออกมาและออกอุบายแกล้งทำเป็น
นอนตายเพื่อให้พวกหนูตายใจ แต่มีหนูตัวหนึ่งรู้ทันว่าแมวกำลังแกล้ง
ตาย จึงค่อย ๆ ย่องออกมาจากรูอย่างช้า ๆ แล้วบอกกับแมวว่า "แมวเจ้า
เล่ห์ พวกข้ารู้ดีว่ามันเป็นกลลวงของเจ้า ข้าและเพื่อน ๆ ไม่เชื่อในอุบาย
ตื้น ๆ ของเจ้าหรอก" พูดจบหนูก็รีบวิ่งกลับเข้ารูตามเดิม

Vocabulary

1	ชุกชุม	**chúk chum**	scores of (a large number of)
2	เจ้าของ	**jâo khǎwng**	owner
3	กำจัด	**gam jàt**	to get rid of
4	สังเกต	**sǎng gèht**	to notice
5	เป็นห่วง	**pen hùang**	to be worried
6	ความปลอดภัย	**khwaam plàwt phai**	safety
7	อาหาร	**aa hǎan**	food
8	รู	**ruu**	hole
9	ห้องครัว	**hǎwng khrua**	kitchen
10	แกล้งตาย	**glâehng taay**	to play dead
11	แผนการ	**phǎehn gaan**	plan
12	หลอกล่อ	**làwk lâw**	to trick
13	ออกอุบาย	**àwk u-baay**	to fool (someone)
14	รู้ทัน	**rúu than**	to realize immediately
15	ย่อง	**yâwng**	to tiptoe
16	เจ้าเล่ห์	**jâo-lêh**	cunning
17	กลลวง	**gon luang**	ruse

Comprehension Questions

1. What did the owner do to get rid of the mice in his house?

2. Where would the remaining mice go in search of food?

3. What did the cat do to fool the mice?

4. How do you say "cat" and "mice" in Thai?

Writing Activity

What would you do if your house were infested with mice?

The Trees and the Ax

Once there was a young man who wanted to cut down a tree to repair his house. But his ax was of no use, as it was missing a handle. So, one day the man took his knife and went tramping into the woods. He slashed at a big tree with the knife, but swing as he might, it would not fall. So, he begged the king of the trees, "May I have a small tree to use as a handle for my ax?"

Although many of the trees in the forest objected, realizing the danger that this would pose, the king allowed the man to use his knife to cut down a small tree. He said to the other trees, "Allow him to go ahead. He will not bother us again."

The young man thus took the small tree he had cut down and fashioned it into a handle for his ax. He then returned to the forest as before. Only this time, he did not come to ask for another tree, but to cut down nearly all of the large trees in the forest. And before the king of the trees was felled, he said to the others, "If only I hadn't given him that small tree to start with, he would not have been able to make a handle for that ax and chop us down!"

ต้นไม้กับขวาน

ชายหนุ่มคนหนึ่งเดินเข้าไปในป่า เขาตั้งใจเข้าไปเพื่อตัดต้นไม้นำมา
ซ่อมแซมบ้าน แต่ขวานที่จะใช้ตัดต้นไม้ใช้งานไม่ได้เพราะไม่มีด้าม วัน
หนึ่งเขาจึงเดินเข้าไปในป่าพร้อมกับมีด แต่ใช้มีดฟันเท่าไรต้นไม้ใหญ่ก็ไม่
ยอมโค่น เขาจึงขอร้องราชาแห่งต้นไม้ใหญ่ในป่าว่า "ข้าขอต้นไม้ต้นเล็ก ๆ
สักต้นเพื่อไปต่อเป็นด้ามขวานได้ไหม"

ถึงแม้ต้นไม้หลายต้นในป่าจะคัดค้านถึงผลเสียที่จะตามมา แต่ราชา
แห่งต้นไม้อนุญาตให้เขาใช้มีดฟันต้นไม้ต้นเล็ก ๆ ไปได้หนึ่งต้น และบอก
กับต้นไม้ต้นอื่น ๆ ว่า "ให้เขาไปเถอะ เขาจะได้ไม่มาวุ่นวายกับเราอีก"

ชายหนุ่มจึงนำต้นไม้ต้นเล็กมาทำเป็นด้ามขวาน แต่เขาก็กลับมายังป่า
อีกเช่นเดิม คราวนี้เขาไม่ได้มาเพื่อขอต้นไม้อีก แต่เขามาเพื่อตัดต้นไม้
ใหญ่ที่อยู่ในป่าจนเกือบหมด และก่อนที่ราชาต้นไม้จะถูกโค่น เขาพูดกับ
ต้นไม้อื่น ๆ ว่า "ถ้าตอนแรกเราไม่ให้ต้นไม้เล็ก ๆ กับเขาไป เขาคงไม่มี
ไม้ไปทำด้ามขวานเพื่อมาโค่นพวกเราได้"

Vocabulary

1	ชายหนุ่ม	**chaay nùm**	young man
2	ป่า	**pàa**	forest
3	ต้นไม้	**tôn mái**	tree
4	ซ่อมแซม	**sâwm saehm**	to fix
5	ขวาน	**khwǎan**	ax
6	ด้าม	**dâam**	handle
7	มีด	**mîit**	knife
8	ขอร้อง	**khǎw ráwng**	to beg
9	ราชา	**raa-chaa**	king
10	คัดค้าน	**khát kháan**	to object
11	อนุญาต	**à-nú-yâat**	to allow
12	ผลเสีย	**phǒn sǐa**	damage
13	วุ่นวาย	**wûn waay**	to bother
14	เช่นเดิม	**chêhn derrm**	as before
15	เกือบ	**gùeap**	nearly
16	หมด	**mòd**	all of (something)
17	โค่น	**khôhn**	to fell
18	อื่น ๆ	**ùehn ùehn**	others

Comprehension Questions

1. Why did the man want to cut down a tree?

2. What did he beg the king of the trees to give to him?

3. How did he use the small tree he had cut down?

4. After he had put a new handle on his ax, what did he do?

Writing Activity

What are some possible effects of cutting down trees?

The Dog and Its Reflection

A dog was lying on the ground, exhausted, as he had not eaten in many days. He decided that in order to survive, he would need to steal a piece of meat from the market. Fortunately for him, he was able to snatch a large slab from a vendor without being caught. He clenched the meat in his jaw and began to trot straight home. As he was crossing a bridge, he looked down and saw his reflection shimmering in the water. He thought, "That dog has an even bigger piece of meat than I do! I have to find a way to take it." He had mistaken his own reflection for another dog with a thicker slice of meat and he greedily wanted it for himself. So, the dog swatted at the reflection with his paws, barking noisily as he did so. This sent the meat he had been carrying in his mouth tumbling into the water. So, aside from not getting another piece, he had lost the one he had previously had. The dog could only stand there on the bridge, feeling discouraged.

Vocabulary

1	สุนัข	sù nák	dog (formal)
2	หมดแรง	mòt raehng	exhausted
3	เพราะ	phráw	as, because
4	หลาย	làay	many
5	ขโมย	khà-mohy	to steal
6	เนื้อ	núea	meat
7	ตลาด	tà làat	market
8	ประทังชีวิต	prà-thang chii-wít	to survive
9	โชคดี	chôhk dii	lucky
10	คาบ	khâap	to clench/carry (in one's mouth)
11	ข้าม	khâam	to cross
12	สะพาน	sà phaan	bridge
13	เงาสะท้อน	ngao sà-tháwn	reflection

สุนัขกับเงา

มีสุนัขตัวหนึ่งกำลังนอนหมดแรงเพราะไม่มีอะไรกินมานานหลายวัน จึง
ไปขโมยเนื้อมาจากตลาดเพื่อประทังชีวิต และโชคดีที่ได้เนื้อชิ้นใหญ่มาโดย
ไม่มีใครจับได้ มันคาบเนื้อชิ้นนั้นไว้ในปากและตรงกลับบ้าน ขณะกำลัง
ข้ามสะพานและมองลงไปเห็นเงาสะท้อนในน้ำ แล้วคิดว่า "สุนัขตัวนั้นมี
ชิ้นเนื้อชิ้นใหญ่กว่าเราอีก ต้องแย่งมาให้ได้" เพราะเข้าใจผิดว่าเป็นสุนัข
อีกตัวหนึ่งที่มีเนื้ออีกชิ้นหนึ่งซึ่งมีขนาดใหญ่กว่า และด้วยความโลภอยาก
ได้เนื้อชิ้นนั้นเช่นกัน เจ้าสุนัขก็เลยเอาเท้าตะปบเงาในน้ำและเห่าเสียงดัง
ซึ่งจังหวะนั้นเองชิ้นเนื้อที่มันคาบอยู่ในปากก็ร่วงตกน้ำไป นอกจากจะไม่
ได้เนื้อเพิ่มอีกชิ้นแล้ว ยังเสียเนื้อในปากไปอีกด้วย เจ้าสุนัขจึงได้แต่ยืน
เสียใจอยู่บนสะพาน

14	เข้าใจผิด	**khâo jai phìt**	to be mistaken
15	อยากได้	**yàak dâi**	to want
16	ความโลภ	**khwaam lôhp**	greedy
17	เสียใจ	**sĭa jai**	discouraged

Comprehension Questions

1. Where did the dog steal the piece of meat from?

2. What did the dog see in the water as he was crossing the bridge?

3. What happened when the dog saw a bigger piece of meat in the reflection?

4. How did the dog feel after he had lost the meat?

Writing Activity

What is the moral of this story?

The Farmer and the Cobra

One morning, a kind farmer went out to work in the field with his neighbor as he did every day. As he and his neighbor set to work, it began to rain heavily. They sought shelter from the rain underneath a large tree, where the farmer caught sight of a cobra lying stiff and motionless on the ground. Upon seeing this, he took pity on the snake. He tried to pick it up and wrap it in his loincloth to warm it. When the cobra came to, it snapped around, bit the kind farmer's arm, and slithered away. The farmer, who was on the brink of death from the cobra's venom, said to his neighbor, "I shouldn't have helped that wicked snake! It's fitting that I should die because of it!" Upon saying this, he died miserably.

ชาวนากับงูเห่า

เช้าวันหนึ่งชาวนาใจดีและเพื่อนบ้านออกไปทำนาเหมือนเช่นเคยทุกวัน
ขณะที่ชาวนากำลังทำนากับเพื่อนบ้านอยู่นั้น ฝนตกลงมาอย่างหนัก เขา
เดินไปใต้ต้นไม้ใหญ่เพื่อหลบฝน แล้วชาวนาก็เหลือบไปเห็นงูเห่าตัวหนึ่ง
นอนแข็งไม่กระดุกกระดิกเลย ชาวนาเห็นแล้วเกิดความสงสาร เขาจึงใช้มือ
อุ้มงูเห่าขึ้นมา แล้วเอาผ้าขาวม้าคลุมงูเห่าไว้เพื่อให้ความอบอุ่น ต่อมางูเห่า
ก็ฟื้นขึ้นมาแล้วหันไปกัดแขนของชาวนาผู้ใจดี จากนั้นงูก็เลื้อยหนีไป ก่อน
ที่จะเลื้อยหนีไป ชาวนาทนพิษงูเห่าไม่ไหวจึงสิ้นใจตายอยู่ตรงนั้น ก่อนตาย
เขาได้บอกเพื่อนบ้านที่มายืนดูว่า "ข้าไม่น่าช่วยสัตว์ร้ายนี้เลย สมควรแล้ว
ที่ข้าจะต้องตายเพราะมัน" พูดจบชาวนาใจดีก็ขาดใจตายอย่างน่าสงสาร

Vocabulary

1	ชาวนา	**chaaw naa**	farmer
2	ใจดี	**jai dii**	kind
3	งูเห่า	**nguu hào**	cobra
4	เพื่อนบ้าน	**phâean bâan**	neighbor
5	ทุกวัน	**thúk wan**	every day
6	ฝน	**fŏn**	rain
7	เหลือบ	**lùeap**	to catch sight of (something)
8	กระดุกกระดิก	**grà dùk grà dìk**	to move
9	สงสาร	**sŏng săan**	to pity
10	อุ้ม	**ûm**	to pick something/someone up
11	ผ้าขาวม้า	**phâa khăaw máa**	loincloth
12	ให้ความอบอุ่น	**hâi khwaam òp ùn**	to warm
13	ฟื้น	**fúehn**	to come to
14	กัด	**gàt**	to bite
15	เลื้อย	**lúeay**	to slither
16	พิษงู	**phít nguu**	venom
17	สัตว์ร้าย	**sàt ráay**	wicked animal

Comprehension Questions

1. What did the farmer and his neighbor do every day?

2. What condition was the cobra in when the farmer saw it?

3. What did the farmer do to warm the cobra?

4. Where did the cobra bite the farmer?

Writing Activity

Write about the dangers of snakes.

The Lion and the Mouse

One day, a lion was sleeping soundly under a large tree, when he was awakened by a mouse scurrying by his leg. The lion immediately arose and pounced, snatching the small mouse in his paw, fully intending to kill it. The mouse pleaded with the lion pitifully, "Dear lion, please spare my life. If you do, one day I will help you in return. Who knows? I may be able to help you within the next two or three days." Upon hearing this, the lion burst out laughing and released the mouse.

Some days later, the lion became caught in a hunter's trap and was ensnared in a rope tied firmly to a tree. He was unable to wriggle free, so he roared, and his roar echoed throughout the forest. When the little mouse heard this, she hastily scampered over to help the lion. While the hunter was away getting something to eat, the mouse gnawed through the ropes wrapped around the lion's foot, thus freeing him. "You see, I told you I would help you someday," she said proudly.

ราชสีห์กับหนู

วันหนึ่งใต้ต้นไม้ใหญ่สิงโตตัวหนึ่งกำลังนอนหลับสบาย แต่ต้องสะดุ้งตื่น
เพราะมีหนูตัวหนึ่งวิ่งผ่านขาของมันไป สิงโตลุกขึ้นแล้วตะปบจับหนูน้อย
ไว้ในอุ้งเท้าทันทีและคิดจะฆ่าหนูให้ตาย หนูอ้อนวอนสิงโตอย่างน่า
สงสารว่า "ท่านสิงโตได้โปรดไว้ชีวิตข้าด้วย แล้วสักวันข้าจะช่วยเหลือท่าน
เป็นการตอบแทน ใครจะรู้ว่าบางทีข้าอาจจะได้ช่วยเหลือท่านภายใน 2-3
วันนี้ก็ได้" สิงโตได้ยินแล้วก็หัวเราะแล้วปล่อยเจ้าหนูไป

จนกระทั่งวันหนึ่ง สิงโตตัวนั้นไปติดกับดักของนายพรานคนหนึ่ง
แล้วถูกล่ามด้วยเชือกที่แข็งแรงไว้กับต้นไม้ ไม่สามารถดิ้นหลุดออกได้
สิงโตจึงส่งเสียงคำรามไปทั่วทั้งป่า เมื่อเจ้าหนูน้อยได้ยินจึงรีบวิ่งมาช่วย
สิงโต ในขณะที่นายพรานออกไปหาอาหาร เจ้าหนูใช้ฟันกัดแทะเชือกที่
ผูกขาของสิงโตไว้จนขาด ทำให้สิงโตเป็นอิสระ "เห็นไหมข้าบอกท่านแล้ว
ว่าสักวันข้าจะช่วยเหลือท่านได้" เจ้าหนูพูดด้วยความภูมิใจ

Vocabulary

1	ราชสีห์, สิงโต	râat chá sǐi (formal), sǐng toh	lion
2	หนู	nǔu	mouse
3	นอนหลับสบาย	nawn-làp sà-baay	to sleep soundly
4	สะดุ้งตื่น	sà dung tùehn	to awaken, to wake (someone) up
5	ตะปบ	tà pòp	to snatch
6	อุ้งเท้า	ûng tháo	paw
7	ฆ่า	khâa	to kill
8	อ้อนวอน	âwn wawn	to plead, beg
9	ได้โปรด	dâi pròht	please
10	ไว้ชีวิต	wái chii wít	to spare someone's life
11	ช่วยเหลือ	chûay lǔea	to help
12	ปล่อย	plàwy	to release
13	ตอบแทน	tàwp thaehn	in return
14	กับดัก	gàp dàk	trap
15	นายพราน	naay phraan	hunter
16	ล่าม	lâam	to ensnare
17	เชือก	chûeak	rope
18	คำราม	kham raam	to roar
19	ทำให้...เป็นอิสระ	tham-hâi.....pen ìt sà rà	to free
20	ภูมิใจ	phuum jai	proud

Comprehension Questions

1. What did the mouse do to awake the lion?
2. Who made the trap?
3. What did the mouse hear before coming to help the lion?
4. How did the mouse help the lion?

Writing Activity

Write about your experience in helping someone in return for a past favor.

The Boy Who Cried Wolf

There was once a goatherd boy who watched over the goats in the foothills near his village. One day, he thought that it would be a lark to play a prank on the villagers and give them a surprise. So, he sprinted to the village yelling "Help! Help! A wolf! It's going to eat the goats!" The villagers all came out to see what had happened, but there was no wolf in sight, only the goatherd boy sitting and laughing mirthfully. On another day, he tried the same ruse again, and the villagers ran out excitedly to help him as before.

Then one day, a wolf actually appeared and began gobbling up the goats, one by one. So, the frightened boy cried out at the top of his lungs, "Help! Help! Wolf! Wolf! Someone please come out and help! The wolf is eating my goats!" But this time, the villagers assumed it was just another one of the goatherd boy's tricks. Thus, no one paid any attention to his cries and no one came to help, allowing the wolf to devour the goatherd boy's flock with ease.

Vocabulary

1	หมู่บ้าน	**mùu bâan**	village
2	เด็กเลี้ยงแพะ	**dèk líang pháe**	goatherd boy
3	เฝ้า	**fâo**	to watch over
4	เชิงเขา	**cherrng khǎo**	foothills
5	นึกสนุก	**núek sà nùk**	lark
6	แกล้ง	**glâehng**	to play a prank
7	ตกใจ	**tòk jai**	surprise
8	หมาป่า	**mǎa pàa**	wolf
9	หัวเราะ	**hǔa ráw**	to laugh
10	กลัว	**glua**	frightened
11	ร้องตะโกน	**ráwng tà-gohn**	to cry out, scream
12	อุบาย	**ù baay**	trick

เด็กเลี้ยงแพะ

หมู่บ้านแห่งหนึ่งมีเด็กเลี้ยงแพะคนหนึ่งคอยเฝ้าฝูงแพะอยู่ที่เชิงเขาใกล้หมู่บ้าน วันหนึ่งเขานึกสนุกอยากแกล้งชาวบ้านให้ตกใจ จึงวิ่งไปที่หมู่บ้านพร้อมกับร้องตะโกนว่า "ช่วยด้วย ๆ หมาป่า! หมาป่า! จะมากินแพะแล้ว" ชาวบ้านพากันออกมาดูว่าเกิดอะไรขึ้น แต่กลับไม่พบหมาป่า มีเพียงเด็กเลี้ยงแพะที่นั่งหัวเราะชอบใจ หลังจากวันนั้นเขาก็ใช้อุบายเดิมอีกครั้ง และชาวบ้านก็วิ่งหน้าตื่นออกมาเพื่อช่วยเหลือเขาเช่นเคย

และแล้วในวันหนึ่งหมาป่าก็มาจริง ๆ และเริ่มกินแพะทีละตัว ๆ เด็กเลี้ยงแพะตกใจกลัวร้องตะโกนสุดเสียง "ช่วยด้วย ๆ หมาป่า! หมาป่า! ใครก็ได้ออกมาช่วยที หมาป่ากำลังกินแพะของข้า" แต่คราวนี้ชาวบ้านต่างคิดว่าเด็กเลี้ยงแพะคงหลอกพวกเขาอีกแล้ว จึงไม่มีใครสนใจเสียงร้องของเขา และไม่มีใครมาช่วยเหลือเขา หมาป่าเลยกินฝูงแพะของเด็กเลี้ยงแพะได้อย่างสบาย

13	อีกครั้ง	**ìik**	again
14	จริง ๆ	**jing jing**	actually
15	แพะ	**pháe**	goat
16	คราวนี้	**khraaw níi**	this time

Comprehension Questions

1. Where did the goatherd boy watch over the goats?
2. What prank did the goatherd boy play on the villagers?
3. What did the goatherd boy do when the villagers came out?
4. What happened when no one came to help the goatherd boy?

Writing Activity

If you were a villager, what advice would you give to the goatherd boy?

The Tortoise and the Hare

One day, a tortoise was plodding slowly along in a large forest when a hare ran swiftly past her from the opposite direction. The hare mocked the tortoise, "How is it even possible that you move so slowly?"

The tortoise replied, "I may move slowly, but when it comes to patience, I am the best there is."

When the hare heard this, he guffawed so loudly that it caused the other animals in the forest to come out and gather around them. The tortoise then asked the hare, "Do you want to try racing me up that mountain? I will surely win."

The hare was confident in his speed and that he would undoubtably beat the tortoise, so he accepted the proposal. A fox from the crowd of animals that had gathered marked the path and finish line.

When the day of the race arrived, the hare and the tortoise took off together from the starting line, the tortoise inching along and the hare dashing briskly forward.

It was not long before the hare had run halfway up the mountain. He turned and saw that the tortoise was still plodding along slowly, far behind him. And so, the overconfident hare decided to rest by the side of the trail. He nodded off quickly, assuming there was no way the tortoise could ever catch up.

While the hare was sound asleep, the tortoise moved steadily forward without thinking of rest. "Although my legs are short and my gait is slow, I must do my best." When she was halfway up the mountain, she heard a snoring sound coming from somewhere nearby. And sure enough, there was the hare, napping peacefully. Meanwhile, the tortoise solemnly and patiently continued forward.

When the hare finally woke, he sprang bolt upright and quickly scanned the path for the tortoise. However, it was too late. As he reached the finish line, he saw that the other animals had already gathered there and were merrily congratulating the tortoise on her victory.

กระต่ายกับเต่า

วันหนึ่งในป่าใหญ่มีเต่าตัวหนึ่งคลานอย่างช้า ๆ และอีกทางด้านหนึ่งก็มี
กระต่ายตัวหนึ่งวิ่งผ่านมาด้วยความรวดเร็ว กระต่ายเยาะเย้ยเต่าว่า "ทำไม
เจ้าถึงได้เดินได้ช้าอย่างนั้น"

เต่าจึงพูดว่า "ถึงแม้ว่าข้าจะเดินช้า แต่ถ้าพูดถึงเรื่องความอดทนแล้ว
ข้าไม่เคยแพ้ใคร"

เมื่อกระต่ายได้ยินก็หัวเราะเสียงดังทำให้สัตว์ที่อยู่แถวนั้นต่างพากัน
ออกมา เต่าถามกลับไปว่า "เจ้าลองมาแข่งวิ่งไปบนยอดเขานั่นกับข้าไหม
ล่ะ ข้าจะชนะเจ้าให้ได้"

กระต่ายเชื่อมั่นในความเร็วของตัวเองและคิดว่าเต่าชนะไม่ได้แน่นอน
จึงยอมรับข้อเสนอนั้น โดยให้สุนัขจิ้งจอกเป็นคนเลือกเส้นทางและ
กำหนดเส้นชัย

เมื่อถึงวันนัดหมาย กระต่ายกับเต่าก็เริ่มต้นพร้อมกัน เต่าค่อย ๆ เดิน
อย่างเชื่องช้า ในขณะที่กระต่ายวิ่งอย่างรวดเร็ว

ไม่นานก็วิ่งมาถึงกลางทางบนภูเขา แล้วจึงหันไปมองเห็นว่าเต่านั้นยัง
คงคลานตามมาอย่างช้า ๆ อยู่ไกล ๆ กระต่ายจึงนอนพักข้างทางอย่างชะล่า
ใจและหลับไปอย่างรวดเร็ว เพราะคิดว่าถึงยังไงเต่าก็ไม่มีทางตามทันได้

ในขณะที่กระต่ายกำลังหลับสนิทอยู่ แต่เต่าเดินมาอย่างไม่คิดที่จะ
หยุดพักผ่อน "ถึงแม้ว่าขาของข้าสั้นเดินได้ช้า แต่ข้าจะต้องทำดีที่สุด
เท่าที่จะทำได้" เมื่อเต่าเดินมาจนถึงกลางทางบนภูเขาก็ได้ยินเหมือนเสียง
กรนจากที่แห่งหนึ่งที่ใกล้ ๆ ตรงนั้นกระต่ายกำลังนอนหลับอยู่อย่างสุข
สบาย ส่วนเต่านั้นยังคงเดินต่อไปทีละก้าวอย่างจริงจังและอดทน

และแล้วกระต่ายก็เริ่มรู้สึกตัวและสะดุ้งตื่นขึ้นมา รีบกวาดสายตามอง
หาเต่า แต่ก็สายไปเสียแล้ว เพราะเมื่อไปที่เส้นชัยที่อยู่บนยอดเขา ก็เห็น
ว่าสัตว์ต่าง ๆ กำลังแสดงความยินดีที่เต่าได้รับชัยชนะอย่างมีความสุข

Vocabulary

1	กระต่าย	**grà tàay**	hare, rabbit
2	เต่า	**tào**	tortoise, turtle
3	คลาน	**khlaan**	to plod
4	เยาะเย้ย	**yáw yéhy**	to mock
5	ความอดทน	**khwaam òt thon**	patience
6	แข่ง	**khàehng**	to race, compete
7	ยอดเขา	**yâwt khǎo**	mountain
8	ชนะ	**chá ná**	to win
9	เชื่อมั่น	**chûea mân**	to be confident
10	รวดเร็ว	**rûat rew**	swift, speedy
11	แน่นอน	**nâeh nawn**	undoubtably
12	สุนัขจิ้งจอก	**sù nák jîng jàwk**	fox
13	ยอมรับ	**yawm ráp**	to accept
14	ข้อเสนอ	**khâw sà-něrr**	proposal
15	เส้นทาง	**sêhn thaang**	path
16	เส้นชัย	**sêhn chai**	finish line
17	พร้อมกัน	**phráwm gan**	together
18	กลางทาง	**glaang thaang**	halfway
19	ชะล่าใจ	**chá-lâa jai**	overconfident
20	ตามทัน	**taam than**	to catch up
21	ดีที่สุด	**dii thîi sùt**	best
22	เสียงกรน	**sǐang gron**	snoring sound
23	จริงจัง	**jing jang**	solemn/serious
24	สะดุ้ง	**sà dûng**	to spring up suddenly
25	กวาดสายตา	**gwàat sǎay taa**	to scan, look at carefully
26	แสดงความยินดี	**sà-daehng khwaam yin-dii**	to congratulate

Culture notes

Winning a race means being the first to cross the finish line, but this does not mean that the winner must be the fastest runner (like the hare). The slower runner (like the tortoise) also has a chance to reach it first. What helps to bring about victory in any competition or challenge is perseverance and not being discouraged.

Comprehension Questions

1. กระต่ายเยาะเย้ยเต่าเพราะอะไร
2. กระต่ายกับเต่าแข่งวิ่งไปที่ไหน
3. ใครเป็นคนเลือกเส้นทางและกำหนดเส้นชัย
4. ทำไมเต่าจึงชนะกระต่าย

Writing Activity

เขียนแสดงความคิดเห็นว่าคุณชอบ "กระต่ายหรือเต่า" มากที่สุด เพราะอะไร

Which character in this story do you like best, the hare or the tortoise, and why?

The Frogs Who Desired a King

A long time ago, a group of frogs lived together in a large pond. They were free and content, with no one to tell them when they could eat or sleep or play, which made the frogs very happy indeed.

One day, the frogs gathered to discuss whether a large group such as theirs ought to have a leader to rule over them. Besides creating order, they reasoned, such a leader could protect them from danger.

All of the frogs agreed, so they went in search of the spirit in the sky and begged him to send them a leader. The spirit knew that the frogs were used to living carefree lives, so he decided that their leader similarly should not be too strict or serious. So, he summoned a log, which plummeted from the sky and landed with a great splash in the pond. This startled the frogs, who frantically plunged into the water. Only after seeing that it was safe did they begin to cautiously emerge.

กบเลือกนาย

เมื่อนานมาแล้วมีกบฝูงหนึ่งอาศัยอยู่ในหนองน้ำใหญ่แห่งหนึ่งอย่างอิสระ
และมีความสุข ไม่มีใครบังคับ กินนอนเล่นได้ตามใจชอบ พวกกบรู้สึกว่า
ช่างมีความสุขสบายเหลือเกิน

วันหนึ่งพวกกบได้นั่งล้อมวงปรึกษากันว่าการอยู่รวมกันเป็นฝูงใหญ่
น่าจะมีหัวหน้าปกครองสักคน นอกจากจะทำให้เกิดความเป็นระเบียบ
เรียบร้อยแล้ว ยังช่วยคุ้มครองอันตรายให้กับพวกกบได้อีกด้วย

กบทั้งหลายต่างมีความเห็นตรงกันจึงพากันไปหาเทวดาเพื่อขอให้ช่วย
ส่งหัวหน้ามาให้ เทวดารู้ว่าพวกกบสุขสบายกันจนเคยตัว ก็เลยนึกอยาก
มีหัวหน้าไปอย่างนั้นเอง ไม่ได้คิดจริงจังอะไร จึงส่งท่อนซุงจากฟ้าตกลงสู่
หนองน้ำเสียงดังโครมใหญ่ พวกกบพากันตกใจกลัวรีบดำน้ำหนีไปหลบ
ใต้น้ำ เมื่อเห็นว่าปลอดภัยแล้วจึงพากันโผล่ขึ้นมา

When the frogs saw the enormous log, they knew that it was the leader the spirit had bestowed upon them. They all were delighted and treated the log with the utmost respect. Not long after, one of the bolder frogs sprang up and perched atop it. Once the others saw that the log did not protest, they too began to leap onto it.

"Our leader is very kind but far too weak. He just floats there dully back and forth, to and fro," one of the frogs irreverently declared. "We should go and ask for a new and stricter leader to rule over us," said another.

The frogs went again to the spirit to beg for a new leader. When the spirit heard their plea, he became angry that the frogs had not been content with their carefree lives. So, this time, he summoned a heron to replace the log as their leader. When the heron descended, he began scooping up the frogs, gobbling them up one by one. The remaining frogs were desperate and went to ask the spirit for a new leader once more.

"When you are not satisfied with the way things are, you must accept the changes for which you ask!" the spirit thundered from above. From then on, the frogs lived alone in fear, knowing that their discontent with their original circumstances had caused this terrible outcome.

พวกกบทั้งหลายเห็นซุงท่อนใหญ่คิดว่าเป็นหัวหน้าที่เทวดาประทาน
มาให้ต่างพากันดีใจและให้ความเคารพท่อนซุงนั้น ต่อมาไม่นานมีกบตัว
หนึ่งใจกล้ากระโดดขึ้นไปเกาะบนท่อนซุงใหญ่ กบตัวอื่น ๆ เห็นว่า
หัวหน้าไม่ว่าอะไรก็พากันกระโดดตามขึ้นไปบ้าง

"หัวหน้าของเราคนนี้ท่านใจดีแต่อ่อนแอไม่เอาไหน วัน ๆ ได้แต่ลอย
ไปลอยมา" กบตัวหนึ่งพูดอย่างไม่มีความยำเกรง "พวกเราน่าจะไปร้องขอ
หัวหน้าใหม่ที่เข้มแข็งกว่านี้มาปกครองพวกเราดีกว่า" กบอีกตัวพูด

กบจึงพากันไปร้องขอต่อเทวดา เทวดาเห็นว่าพวกกบทำแบบนั้นจึง
โกรธที่ไม่รู้จักพอใจในความเป็นอยู่ที่สุขสบายของตน ครั้งนี้เลยส่งนก
กระสาไปแทนท่อนซุง เมื่อนกกระสาลงไปก็จับพวกกบกินเป็นอาหารตัว
แล้วตัวเล่า พวกกบหายไปทีละตัว ๆ เมื่อได้รับความเดือดร้อน พวกกบที่
เหลืออยู่จึงพากันขอหัวหน้าใหม่จากเทวดาอีกครั้ง

"เมื่อเจ้าไม่พอใจความเป็นอยู่เดิมของตัวเองก็ต้องยอมรับสภาพที่พวก
เจ้าร้องขอไปเถอะ" เทวดาตวาดเสียงดังลงมาจากฟากฟ้า กบในฝูงต่างอยู่
ด้วยความกลัว แล้วคิดว่าควรพึงพอใจในสิ่งที่ได้มาตั้งแต่แรก ไม่ควร
ร้องขอสิ่งใดให้มากเรื่องจนเกิดผลร้ายตามมา

Vocabulary

1	กบ	**gòp**	frog
2	ฝูง	**fŭung**	a group of (animals)
3	หนองน้ำ	**năwng náam**	pond
4	อิสระ	**ìt-sà-rà**	free
5	มีความสุข	**mii khwaam-sùk**	happy
6	ล้อมวง	**láwm wong**	to gather
7	ปรึกษา	**prùek săa**	to discuss
8	หัวหน้า	**hŭa nâa**	leader
9	ปกครอง	**pòk khrawng**	to rule over
10	ระเบียบ	**rá bìap**	order (harmonious conditions in society)
11	คุ้มครอง	**khúm khrawng**	to protect
12	เทวดา	**theh wá daa**	spirit
13	ขอ	**khăw**	to beg
14	ส่ง/ประทาน	**sòng / prà than**	to summon
15	ท่อนซุง	**thâwn sung**	log
16	ความเคารพ	**khwaam khao-róp**	respect
17	กระโดด	**grà dòht**	to spring up
18	อ่อนแอ	**àwn aeh**	weak
19	เข้มแข็ง	**khêhm khăeng**	strict
20	นกกระสา	**nók grà săa**	heron
21	ตวาด	**tà wàat**	to thunder, shout
22	พึงพอใจ	**phueng phaw jai**	to be content
23	เดือดร้อน	**dùeat ráwn**	desperate
24	ยอมรับ	**yawm ráp**	to accept
25	ร้องขอ	**ráwng khăw**	to ask

| 26 | ความกลัว | **khwaam glua** | fear |
| 27 | ผลร้าย | **phǒn ráay** | terrible outcome |

Culture Notes

The "Frogs Who Desired a King" is one of Aesop's Fables and warns against being picky and thinking only of satisfying one's immediate desires. When one is too choosy, one may end up getting something worse than one originally had. As with the frogs in the story, such behavior may even be dangerous!

Comprehension Questions

1. ฝูงกบอาศัยอยู่ที่ไหน
2. ฝูงกบขออะไรจากเทวดา
3. เทวดาส่งอะไรมาให้ฝูงกบบ้าง
4. ฝูงกบได้รับความเดือดร้อนหรือผลร้ายอย่างไร

Writing Activity

เขียนบทสนทนาสั้น ๆ ที่ฝูงกบร้องขอเทวดาให้ช่วยส่งหัวหน้ามาให้

Write a short conversation that the frogs and the spirit might have when they beg him to send them a leader.

The Spirit and the Woodcutter

There once was a poor man who lived at the edge of a forest, into which he would often hike and chop down trees to sell as firewood. One day, he took his ax into the woods to cut down a tree on the bank of a river. As he was hacking at the tree, he suddenly slipped, and his ax flew out of his hand and landed with a splash in the river. He dove beneath the water and searched long and hard, but the ax was nowhere to be found. The woodcutter slumped down on the bank and began to weep.

The spirit of the river overheard the man's sobbing and appeared before him. "Why are you crying?" he asked.

The woodcutter replied, "My ax flew into the water and I cannot find it. I do not know what to do without an ax to chop wood."

The spirit said, "Do not worry, I will find your ax for you." Then he threw himself into the river. He returned to the surface with an ax made of gold, which he presented to the woodcutter. "Here is your ax."

เทวดากับคนตัดไม้

ชายคนหนึ่งเป็นคนจนบ้านอยู่ใกล้ป่า เขาเข้าป่าไปตัดไม้มาทำฟืนขายอยู่
ประจำ วันหนึ่งเขาถือขวานเข้าไปตัดไม้ในป่าซึ่งอยู่บนฝั่งแม่น้ำ เมื่อเขา
กำลังตัดไม้อยู่นั้น เขาพลาดทำขวานหลุดมือกระเด็นตกลงไปในแม่น้ำ
เขาดำน้ำงมหาขวานอยู่นานก็ไม่เจอ จึงนั่งร้องไห้อยู่บนฝั่งแม่น้ำ

เทวดาแห่งแม่น้ำได้ยินเสียงเขาร้องไห้ จึงปรากฏตัวขึ้นแล้วพูดว่า "
ทำไมเจ้าจึงร้องไห้"

คนตัดไม้ตอบว่า "ขวานของข้ากระเด็นลงน้ำไป หาไม่เจอ ไม่รู้ว่าจะทำ
อย่างไรเพราะข้าไม่มีขวานจะตัดฟืนต่อไป"

เทวดาจึงบอกว่า "ไม่เป็นไร ข้าจะงมขวานนั้นขึ้นมาให้" ว่าแล้วเทวดา
ก็กระโจนลงน้ำ งมเอาขวานทองคำขึ้นมาส่งให้เขาและพูดว่า "นี่ไง ขวาน
ของเจ้า"

The woodcutter, seeing that this was not his ax, said, "This one is not mine." The river spirit then laid the ax down and dove into the water once again, coming up this time with an ax made of silver. The woodcutter told the river spirit that this was also not his, so he plunged beneath the surface once again, returning, at last, with the woodcutter's ax. When he saw this, he was delighted and said excitedly, "That is it! That is my ax! Please give it to me!" Then, seeing that the woodcutter was an honest man, the spirit allowed him to take the gold and silver axes in addition to the one that he had lost.

When he returned home, he told his neighbor about his encounter with the river spirit and about the gold and silver axes he had received from him. After hearing this, his neighbor headed out to the bank of the same river and started chopping at a tree. After four or five swings, he pretended to slip and flung his ax into the water. He then plopped down onto the ground and began to cry. When the river spirit appeared, the man begged him to help him find his ax. The spirit dove into the water and retrieved an ax of gold. "Is this your ax?"

The greedy woodcutter hurriedly replied, "Yes! Yes! That is my ax!"

Hearing what he knew to be a lie, the river spirit said, "You are a deceitful man, and you speak untruthfully. This ax is not yours." He thus returned the golden ax to the river and disappeared. Not only did the man fail to obtain the golden ax, but he lost his own as well.

คนตัดไม้มองดูขวานเห็นว่าไม่ใช่ของตัวจึงพูดว่า "ไม่ใช่ ขวานนี้ไม่ใช่ของข้า" เทวดาก็วางขวานนั้นไว้ แล้วดำน้ำเอาขวานเงินขึ้นมาส่งให้ คนตัดไม้บอกว่าไม่ใช่ของเขา เทวดาก็ดำน้ำลงไปอีกครั้งและครั้งนี้เทวดาก็ถือขวานของเขาขึ้นมา พอคนตัดไม้เห็นขวานของตัวเองก็ดีใจ จึงพูดขึ้นทันทีว่า "นี่แหละขวานของฉัน ขอให้ฉันเถอะ" เทวดาจึงเอาขวานให้คนตัดไม้รวมทั้งขวานทองคำและขวานเงิน เพราะเห็นว่าเขาเป็นคนซื่อตรงไม่โกหก

เมื่อเขาไปถึงบ้านจึงเล่าเรื่องขวานทองคำและขวานเงินให้เพื่อนบ้านฟัง ชายคนหนึ่งเมื่อได้ฟังเรื่องนั้น ก็ถือขวานไปฟันต้นไม้บนฝั่งแม่น้ำนั้น พอฟันได้สี่ห้าครั้ง เขาก็แกล้งทำให้ขวานกระเด็นตกน้ำและนั่งร้องไห้อยู่ตรงนั้น เทวดาก็ออกมาหา ชายคนนั้นก็อ้อนวอนขอให้เทวดาช่วยงมขวานให้ เทวดางมขวานทองคำขึ้นมา และถามว่า "นี่ขวานของเจ้าใช่หรือไม่"

ชายตัดไม้ผู้โลภมากก็รีบตอบรับในทันทีว่า "ใช่ ๆ ขวานเล่มนี้เป็นของข้า" เทวดาได้ยินแล้วก็รู้ว่าเขาโกหก เทวดาจึงบอกว่า "เจ้าเป็นคนไม่ซื่อตรง ขวานนี้ไม่ใช่ของเจ้า เจ้าพูดไม่จริง" จึงโยนขวานทองคำลงไปในแม่น้ำ แล้วเทวดาก็หายไป เขาไม่ได้ขวานทองคำ แต่ยังต้องเสียขวานของตัวอีกด้วย

Vocabulary

1	คนตัดไม้	**khon tàt mái**	woodcutter
2	คนจน	**khon jon**	poor man
3	ฟืน	**fuehn**	firewood
4	ขาย	**khăay**	to sell
5	ประจำ	**prà jam**	often
6	ฝั่งแม่น้ำ	**fàng mâeh náam**	the bank of a river
7	ขวาน	**khwăn**	ax
8	พลาด	**phlâat**	to slip
9	กระเด็น	**grà den**	to fly out (of one's hand)
10	งม	**ngom**	to search (beneath the water)
11	ร้องไห้	**ráwng hâi**	to weep
12	ปรากฏตัว	**praa gòt tua**	to appear
13	ไม่เป็นไร	**mâi pen rai**	do not worry
14	กระโจน	**grà john**	throw oneself into something
15	ทองคำ	**thawng kham**	gold
16	เงิน	**ngerrn**	silver
17	ซื่อตรง	**sûeh trong**	honest
18	โกหก	**goh hòk**	to lie
19	ดีใจ	**dii jai**	delighted
20	เพื่อนบ้าน	**phûean bâan**	neighbor
21	แกล้ง	**glâehng**	to pretend
22	อ้อนวอน	**âwn wawn**	to beg
23	โลภ	**lôhp**	greedy
24	ไม่จริง	**mâi jing**	untruthful
25	หายไป	**hăay pai**	to disappear
26	ทันที	**than thii**	hurriedly/immediately
27	เสีย	**sĭa**	to lose

Culture Notes

In the past, Thai people believed that large trees were inhabited by spirits. There are two different kinds of spirits: those who have a *vimana* (mythological flying palace or chariot) on top of the tree, and those who do not. Spirits with a *vimana* place it in the crown of the tree, while those who do not live on the branches of the tree. These branches should not be cut, as it would destroy the dwelling place of the spirit. If a tree suspected to host a spirit needs to be felled, it is best to pray first in order to invoke the spirit and allow it to find a new dwelling place first.

Comprehension Questions

1. คนตัดไม้นั่งร้องไห้ที่ไหน
2. ทำไมคนตัดไม้จึงร้องไห้
3. เทวดาให้อะไรกับคนตัดไม้
4. เมื่อรู้ว่าชายเพื่อนบ้านโกหก เทวดาทำอะไร

Writing Activity

เขียนบทสนทนาระหว่างคนตัดไม้กับเพื่อนบ้านพูดถึงขวานทองคำและขวานเงินที่ได้จากเทวดา

Write a dialogue between the woodcutter and his neighbor where he recounts the meeting with the river spirit and how he was given the golden and silver axes.

The Wind and the Sun

One fine, clear day, the sun was out and shining as usual when her long-time friend, the wind, swept by. When the wind saw the sun, he stopped. "How are you, Sun? It's been a while!" he bellowed out to his old friend. The sun responded happily, having not seen the wind in ages.

Just then, the wind saw a young, cloaked traveler ambling along below. This gave him an amusing idea for a challenge. "Sun, my friend, how about a contest to see which one of us is the most powerful?" he prodded cajolingly.

"Sure. What kind of contest?" the sun replied without thinking.

The wind gestured down at the traveler and said, "It'll be easy. We'll try any way we can to get that young man's cloak to come off. Whichever one of us is able to do it will be the winner and, thus, the strongest."

ลมกับพระอาทิตย์

ในวันหนึ่งที่ท้องฟ้าแจ่มใสพระอาทิตย์ออกมาส่องแสงอย่างที่เคยเป็น ลม
เพื่อนเก่าได้ผ่านมาเห็นเลยหยุดแวะทักทาย "เป็นอย่างไรบ้างพระอาทิตย์
ไม่เจอกันนานสบายดีไหม" ลมตะโกนทักทายเพื่อนเก่าสุดเสียง
พระอาทิตย์ก็ตอบรับอย่างดีใจเพราะไม่เจอลมมานาน

ขณะนั้นเองมีชายหนุ่มนักเดินทางสวมเสื้อคลุมกำลังเดินเล่นอยู่ ลม
เห็นอย่างนั้นก็นึกสนุก พูดท้าทายออกมา "พระอาทิตย์เพื่อนรัก เรามา
แข่งขันวัดความแข็งแกร่งกันไหม" ลมพูดชักชวน

"ได้สิ แข่งอะไรล่ะ" พระอาทิตย์ตอบกลับแบบไม่คิดอะไร

ลมชี้ไปยังหนุ่มนักเดินทางคนนั้นพร้อมพูดว่า "ง่ายมากเลย ทำยังไง
ก็ได้ให้เสื้อคลุมของหนุ่มคนนั้นหลุดออกมาจากตัว ใครทำสำเร็จถือเป็นผู้
ชนะและแข็งแกร่งที่สุด"

The sun nodded in response. When the wind saw that his friend had accepted the challenge, he swooped down toward the traveler, shouting behind him, "I'll go first!"

The wind gathered up all of his strength into a small storm so as to sweep the cloak up and off the traveler. But the young man was not shaken. On the contrary, this caused him to gather his cloak even tighter around him. When the wind saw this, he forced himself to become even stronger, until the traveler was barely able to compel his feet forward against its resistance. "Why is the wind so strong today?" he complained dejectedly and pulled his cloak tighter still around him. So, the wind summoned his strength once more and blew so hard that the traveler staggered and nearly fell.

"That's enough, Wind. Let me give it try!" said the sun. The wind's strength was almost completely exhausted, so he allowed the sun to have his turn. Suddenly, the weather cleared and the storm disappeared. The young traveler continued to walk until he neared a row of trees. Then, the sun began to carry out her plan, slowly emerging and shining a bit brighter, then a bit brighter still, until the air became hot and stifling. Warmth gave way to sweltering heat, making the traveler too hot to continue walking. When he reached the serene line of trees, he decided to sit and rest. He then removed his cloak and set it beside him, thus cinching the sun's victory.

The wind was pleased with what the sun had done. "Someday we'll meet again, Sun, my friend!" The two of them smiled and bade each other a cheerful farewell.

พระอาทิตย์พยักหน้าตอบรับ เมื่อเพื่อนรักรับคำท้าลมจึงโผไปหาหนุ่ม
นักเดินทาง แล้วตะโกนไล่หลัง "ฉันขอเริ่มก่อนนะ"

ลมรวบรวมพลังทั้งหมดเป็นพายุขนาดย่อม หวังทำให้เสื้อคลุมตัวนั้น
ปลิว แต่หนุ่มนักเดินทางไม่หวั่นไหวถคมยังจับเสื้อคลุมให้กระชับตัวมาก
ขึ้น ลมเห็นอย่างนั้นก็ยิ่งใช้แรงบีบบังคับมากขึ้นไปอีก จนหนุ่มคนนั้น
แทบไม่มีแรงก้าวเดิน "ทำไมวันนี้ลมแรงนักนะ" หนุ่มนักเดินทางบ่น
อย่างท้อใจแล้วดึงเสื้อคลุมแน่นกว่าเดิม ลมจึงรวบรวมพลังอีกครั้งพร้อม
กับเป่าไปยังหนุ่มคนนั้นจนเขาเดินเซเกือบล้ม

"พอเถอะลม เราขอลองแข่งบ้าง" พระอาทิตย์บอกกับลม ด้วยแรงที่
ใกล้จะหมด ลมจึงยอมให้พระอาทิตย์มาแข่งต่อ คราวนี้อากาศแจ่มใสไม่มี
พายุ หนุ่มนักเดินทางเลยเดินต่อจนใกล้ถึงแนวป่า ด้านพระอาทิตย์เองก็
เริ่มแผนการค่อย ๆ ออกมาส่องแสงสว่างทีละนิดจนอากาศร้อนอบอ้าว
จากความอบอุ่นกลายเป็นความร้อน ทำให้หนุ่มนักเดินทางเริ่มรู้สึกร้อน
เกินกว่าจะเดินต่อไป พอถึงแนวต้นไม้เงียบสงบ หนุ่มนักเดินทางเลย
เลือกที่จะเข้าไปนั่งพักพร้อมถอดเสื้อคลุมวางไว้ข้างกาย ในที่สุด
พระอาทิตย์ก็เป็นฝ่ายชนะ

ลมชื่นชมในสิ่งที่พระอาทิตย์ทำ "เราจะแวะมาหาใหม่นะพระอาทิตย์
เพื่อนรัก" ทั้งคู่ยิ้มลากันอย่างมีความสุข

Vocabulary

1	ท้องฟ้าแจ่มใส	**tháwng fáa jàehm săi**	bright and clear sky
2	พระอาทิตย์	**phrá aa thít**	sun
3	ส่องแสง	**sàwng săehng**	shining
4	เพื่อนเก่า	**phûean gào**	long-time friend
5	ตะโกนทักทาย	**tà-gohn thák thaay**	to bellow out, shout a greeting
6	นักเดินทาง	**nák derrn thaang**	traveler
7	เสื้อคลุม	**sûea khlum**	cloak
8	เดินเล่น	**derrn lêhn**	to amble along, stroll
9	นึกสนุก	**núek sà nùk**	to have an amusing idea
10	ท้าทาย	**tháa thaay**	challenge
11	แข็งแกร่ง	**khăeng raehng**	powerful
12	หลุด	**lùt**	to come off
13	ผู้ชนะ	**phûu chá-ná**	winner
14	รวบรวม	**rûap ruam**	to gather
15	พายุ	**phaa yú**	storm
16	ปลิว	**pliw**	to sweep/blow away
17	กระชับ	**grà cháp**	tight
18	บีบบังคับ	**bìip bang-kháp**	to force
19	บ่น	**bòn**	to complain
20	ท้อใจ	**tháw jai**	dejected
21	หมด(แรง)	**mòt (raehng)**	completely exhausted
22	เป่า	**pào**	to blow
23	เดินเซ	**derrn seh**	to stagger
24	ทีละนิด	**thii lá nít**	little by little
25	ร้อนอบอ้าว	**ráwn òp âaw**	hot and stifling

26	ความอบอุ่น	khwaam òp ùn	warm
27	เงียบสงบ	ngîap sà-ngòp	serene
28	ถอด	thàwt	to remove
29	ชื่นชม	chûehn chom	to be pleased with

Culture Notes

This story teaches that brute physical force does not always get us what we want. Sometimes acting aggressively may actually backfire and have the opposite effect of what was intended. Instead, we may be more successful if we use more gentle and cooperative means to achieve our goals.

Comprehension Questions

1. ลมกับพระอาทิตย์แข่งขันทำอะไร
2. ใครเริ่มแข่งขันก่อน
3. หนุ่มนักเดินทางนั่งพักที่ไหน
4. ใครเป็นผู้ชนะ

Writing Activity

เขียนคำหรือประโยคใหม่ที่ได้จากการอ่านเรื่องนี้

Make a list of new or interesting words or phrases you found in this story.

The Salt Merchant and His Donkey

There was once a salt merchant who would regularly pack his salt onto the back of his trusty donkey and haul it around to various cities to sell. One day during his travels, the donkey, whose back was laden with salt, began feeling extremely tired. "Ah, why does the road feel so terribly long and this salt so terribly heavy today?"

But the salt merchant continued pulling the donkey along without rest. Their path on that day led them over a stream. As they were walking across—due to either the weight of his burden or to his own fatigue—the donkey's foot landed on a stone, which caused him to stumble and topple over into the stream. He lay there miserably on his back until the salt merchant was able to pull him out. The fall had caused some of the salt from his load to dissolve into the water.

พ่อค้าเกลือกับลา

มีพ่อค้าเกลือคนหนึ่งบรรทุกเกลือใส่หลังลาคู่ใจเพื่อนำไปขายตามเมือง
ต่าง ๆ อยู่เป็นประจำ วันหนึ่งขณะที่กำลังเดินทาง ลาของเขาที่แบกถุง
เกลือเต็มหลังรู้สึกหนักและเหนื่อยอย่างที่สุด มันจึงบ่นว่า "โอ๊ย วันนี้
ทำไมถึงรู้สึกว่าไกลและหนักอย่างนี้"

    แต่พ่อค้าเกลือก็ยังคงเดินจูงไปเรื่อย ๆ ไม่ยอมหยุด วันนี้เขาต้องพาลา
ข้ามลำธารแห่งหนึ่ง ขณะกำลังเดินข้ามอยู่นั้น จะด้วยความหนักของถุง
เกลือหรือว่าความเหนื่อยก็ไม่รู้ ลาก้าวขาเหยียบหินสะดุดล้มและตกลงไป
ในลำธาร นอนหงายอย่างไม่เป็นท่า กว่าพ่อค้าจะเข้ามาช่วยและลากมัน
ขึ้นมาจากน้ำได้ ทำให้เกลือที่บรรทุกอยู่บนหลังบางส่วนได้ละลายไปกับน้ำ

"Oh no! Do you see? All of this salt has all dissolved!" the salt merchant complained angrily, turning and scolding the donkey. But once the donkey arose, he felt that his burden had eased considerably. This taught him that falling into the water would earn him a lighter load.

From that day onward, whenever the merchant and his salt-laden donkey reached a stream or pond, the donkey would feign tripping and fall into the water. The salt would then inevitably dissolve, which would cause great losses for the merchant.

After a few such incidents, the merchant sat and pondered the matter. He immediately realized the donkey's ruse. The tricky animal had surely been putting one over on him and would need to be taught a lesson.

One day, instead of salt, the merchant filled his bags with a load of cotton of equal weight. The donkey was unaware of the merchant's ploy, and when next they reached a stream, he fell over and lay in the water as usual. However, when the cotton became wet, it absorbed the water and became many times heavier than before, thus forcing him to shoulder a much heavier load on the trip back home. After that, the cunning donkey never again dared pretend to stumble into the water.

"โอ๊ย แย่แล้ว เห็นไหมเกลือละลายหมดเลย" พ่อค้าเกลือบ่นอย่างหัว
เสียแล้วหันมาดุด่าลาด้วยความโกรธ แต่เมื่อลาลุกขึ้นมาก็รู้สึกว่าของที่
บรรทุกมาน้ำหนักเบากว่าเดิมมาก มันจึงจำไว้ว่าถ้าหากตกลงไปในน้ำแล้ว
จะทำให้ของที่บรรทุกอยู่บนหลังเบาลงได้

ตั้งแต่นั้นมาเมื่อพ่อค้าเกลือจูงลาบรรทุกเกลือไปขาย เมื่อถึงลำธารหรือ
หนองน้ำ ลาจะแกล้งล้มและลงไปนอนในน้ำทุกครั้ง และแน่นอนเกลือก็
จะละลายไปกับสายน้ำ ทำให้พ่อค้าเกลือได้รับความเสียหายอย่างมาก

เขามานั่งไตร่ตรองและรู้ทันความเจ้าเล่ห์ของลาว่าขี้โกงและแกล้งเขา
อย่างแน่นอน เขาจะต้องสั่งสอนเสียแล้ว

วันหนึ่งเขาจึงแกล้งเอานุ่นบรรทุกลงไปในถุงให้มีน้ำหนักเท่าเกลือ
ฝ่ายลานั้นไม่รู้ถึงอุบาย เมื่อไปถึงลำธารก็ใช้วิธีเดิม ล้มลงไปนอนในน้ำ
เช่นเคย เมื่อนุ่นถูกน้ำก็อุ้มน้ำเอาไว้ ทำให้หนักมากขึ้นกว่าเดิมหลายเท่า
มันจึงต้องทนแบกของที่หนักขึ้นกว่าเดิมเดินทางกลับบ้าน ทำให้ลาขี้โกง
ไม่กล้าล้มลงไปนอนในน้ำอีกเลย

Vocabulary

1	พ่อค้า	**phâw kháa**	merchant
2	เกลือ	**gluea**	salt
3	ลา	**laa**	donkey
4	บรรทุก	**ban thúk**	to pack, load
5	คู่ใจ	**khûu jai**	trusty
6	เมืองต่าง ๆ	**mueang tàang tàang**	various cities
7	แบก	**bàehk**	to carry, shoulder (a burden)
8	เหนื่อย	**nùeay**	tired
9	หนัก	**nàk**	heavy
10	จูง	**juung**	to pull along
11	เรื่อย ๆ	**rûeay rûeay**	continually
12	ข้าม	**khâam**	over, across
13	ลำธาร	**lam-thaan**	a stream
14	สะดุดล้ม	**sà-dùt lóm**	to stumble
15	พลัดตก	**phlát tòk**	to topple
16	ละลาย	**lá laay**	to dissolve
17	แย่แล้ว	**yâeh láehw**	Oh no!
18	หัวเสีย, โกรธ	**hŭa sĭa, gròht**	angry
19	ดุด่า	**dù dàa**	to scold
20	เบา	**bao**	light (not heavy)
21	แกล้ง	**glâehng**	to feign
22	ความเสียหาย	**khwaam sĭa hăay**	loss
23	ไตร่ตรอง	**trài trawng**	to ponder
24	รู้ทัน	**rúu than**	to realize immediately
25	เจ้าเล่ห์	**jâo lêh**	tricky, cunning

26	สั่งสอน	sàng sǎwn	to teach (someone) a lesson
27	นุ่น	nûn	cotton
28	หลายเท่า	lǎay thâo	many times (as in multiplied)
29	กล้า	glâa	to dare

Culture Notes

The main idea of this story relates to the Thai proverb, "**hâi thúk gàeh thânn thúk nán thǔeng tua**" (what goes around comes around). It means that the harm we cause to others will eventually come back to us. In other words, if we make another person suffer, we will end up suffering too. It helps to remind us that we should not inflict suffering on someone else.

Comprehension Questions

1. พ่อค้าบรรทุกเกลือใส่หลังลาเพื่อไปทำอะไร
2. ทำไมลาสะดุดล้มและตกลงไปในลำธาร
3. ลารู้สึกอย่างไรเมื่อเกลือที่บรรทุกอยู่บนหลังละลายไปกับน้ำ
4. พ่อค้าใส่อะไรลงไปในถุงให้มีน้ำหนักเท่ากับเกลือ

Writing Activity

เขียนข้อความสั้น ๆ หรืออีเมล์ถึงเพื่อนเพื่อแนะนำให้อ่านนิทานเรื่องนี้
Write a short note or email to a friend recommending this story.

The Frightened Rabbit

There was once a vast forest, where animals of all species lived together peacefully. One day, a rabbit was settling down contentedly beneath a coconut tree for his afternoon nap, when all of the sudden, a loud thundering sound jolted him awake. "What was that terribly frightening sound?" The rabbit figured that it must have been a landslide, so he exclaimed at the top of his voice, "A landslide! It's a landslide!" as he leapt to his feet and ran for his life without so much as a glance behind him.

The other rabbits saw him fleeing as if his life depended on it and shouted to him, "What are you running from?" He hollered back, "Hurry! Run! It's a landslide!" After that, a group of panic-stricken rabbits numbering in the hundreds were bounding along behind him, bellowing all the way, "A landslide! A landslide! Everybody run!"

As the other animals in the forest heard this, they, too, took off running after the rabbits. The great lion saw all of the animals large and small racing toward her, kicking up clouds of dust that blanketed the forest. She called out, "What are you all running from?"

They shouted back, "Great Lion, there is a landslide over there, so we are running for our lives!" and continued to flee. Unknown to them, they were rushing directly toward a steep cliff. The lion, showing compassion for all of the animals about to fall to their deaths, ran in front of the group and roared loudly three times. This startled the animals and brought them to their senses, and they stopped in their tracks.

The lion then inquired, "Who among you saw this landslide?"

The animals said, "The elephants saw it!"

The elephants said, "The tigers saw it!"

The tigers said, "The rhinoceroses saw it!"

The rhinoceroses said, "The buffalo saw it!"

The buffalo said, "The boars saw it!"

The boars said, "The deer saw it!"

The deer said, "The rabbits saw it!"

กระต่ายตื่นตูม

ในป่ากว้างใหญ่สัตว์หลายชนิดอาศัยอยู่ด้วยกันอย่างสงบสุข วันหนึ่ง
กระต่ายออกหากินอิ่มแล้ว จึงกลับมานอนพักผ่อนใต้ต้นมะพร้าวอย่าง
เพลิดเพลิน ทันใดนั้นมีเสียงดังสนั่นทำให้กระต่ายตื่นขึ้นมาด้วยความ
ตกใจ "เสียงอะไรทำไมน่ากลัวจัง" กระต่ายคิดว่าเป็นเสียงแผ่นดินถล่ม
จึงร้องสุดเสียงว่า "แผ่นดินถล่มแล้ว ๆ" พร้อมกับกระโดดวิ่งหนีสุดชีวิต
โดยไม่เหลียวหลังมาดูเลย

กระต่ายตัวอื่นเห็นมันวิ่งหนีอะไรมาอย่างสุดชีวิต จึงร้องถามว่า "เจ้า
วิ่งหนีอะไรมา" กระต่ายร้องตอบว่า "รีบหนีเร็ว แผ่นดินถล่มแล้ว ๆ"
จากนั้นฝูงกระต่ายนับร้อยก็รีบวิ่งตามไปด้วยความตื่นกลัวพร้อมช่วยกัน
ตะโกนตลอดทางว่า "แผ่นดินถล่ม! แผ่นดินถล่ม! ทุกคนรีบหนีเร็ว"

สัตว์อื่นในป่าเมื่อได้ยินต่างก็วิ่งหนีตามฝูงกระต่ายไป สิงโตเห็นสัตว์น้อย
ใหญ่วิ่งกันฝุ่นฟุ้งกระจายไปทั่วป่าจึงร้องถามว่า "พวกเจ้าวิ่งหนีอะไรกันมา"

ฝูงกระต่ายตอบกลับไปว่า "ท่านสิงโตแผ่นดินที่โน่นถล่มแล้ว พวกเรา
วิ่งหนีตายกันมา" แล้วก็วิ่งไปต่อมุ่งหน้าไปทางหน้าผาสูงชันโดยไม่รู้ตัว
สิงโตผู้มีเมตตาเกรงว่าสัตว์ทั้งหลายจะตกเหวตายกันหมด จึงวิ่งไปดักข้าง
หน้าพร้อมกับคำรามด้วยเสียงดัง 3 ครั้ง สัตว์ทั้งหลายพอได้ยินเสียงของ
สิงโตก็พากันตกใจกลัว แล้วตื่นจากภวังค์พร้อมกับหยุดวิ่ง

สิงโตจึงถามว่า "ใครเห็นแผ่นดินถล่มบ้าง"

พวกสัตว์บอกว่า "ช้างเห็น"

ช้างบอกว่า "เสือเห็น"

เสือบอกว่า "แรดเห็น"

แรดบอกว่า "ควายเห็น"

ควายบอกว่า "หมูป่าเห็น"

หมูป่าบอกว่า "กวางเห็น"

กวางบอกว่า "กระต่ายเห็น"

The rabbits then pointed and said, "That rabbit saw the landslide!"

The lion asked the rabbit if this was true, to which he replied, "I really heard it, Your Greatness! I was napping underneath a coconut tree, and there was a sound so thunderous that I immediately sprang to my feet and ran for my life!"

The lion told the animals to wait there so that she could discover the truth. "Take me to the place from where the sound came," she said fearlessly, her tone full of strength. The rabbit promptly led the lion to where he had heard the thunderous clamor. "It was beneath that coconut tree that I heard it," the rabbit's voice trembled with fright as he spoke.

Upon hearing this, the lion strode bravely over to the tree. She then shook it with her powerful paws until a coconut came crashing loudly to the ground. "The 'landslide' you heard was nothing but a falling coconut. From now on, if something like this happens, you should investigate the source of the sound. Do not panic and cause the others alarm," the concerned lion instructed the rabbit.

The lion then went back and told all of the animals the truth, after which they dispersed and returned to their homes.

พวกกระต่ายจึงชี้บอกว่า "กระต่ายตัวนี้เห็นแผ่นดินถล่มครับ"

สิงโตจึงถามกระต่ายตัวนั้นว่าจริงไหม กระต่ายตอบว่า "ข้าได้ยินจริง ๆ ท่าน ขณะที่ข้ากำลังนอนพักผ่อนอยู่ใต้ต้นมะพร้าว จู่ ๆ ก็เกิดเสียงดังสนั่นจนข้าตกใจรีบวิ่งหนีตายมา"

เพื่อตรวจสอบข้อเท็จจริง สิงโตจึงบอกให้สัตว์ทั้งหลายรออยู่ก่อน "เจ้าพาข้าไปดูหน่อยว่าเจ้าได้ยินเสียงนั้นมาจากตรงไหน" สิงโตผู้กล้าหาญเอ่ยขึ้นด้วยน้ำเสียงที่เข้มแข็ง กระต่ายจึงรีบพาสิงโตไปดูบริเวณที่เกิดเสียงฟ้าถล่ม "ใต้ต้นมะพร้าวนั่นไงท่านที่ข้าได้ยินเสียงแผ่นดินถล่ม" กระต่ายพูดด้วยน้ำเสียงหวาดกลัว

เมื่อได้ยินเช่นนั้นสิงโตก็เดินเข้าไปอย่างกล้าหาญ แล้วใช้เท้าอันแข็งแรงเขย่าต้นมะพร้าวจนลูกมะพร้าวร่วงลงมาเสียงดัง "เสียงแผ่นดินถล่มที่เจ้าได้ยินเป็นเสียงของลูกมะพร้าวที่ตกกระทบพื้นยังไงล่ะ คราวหน้าหากเกิดอะไรขึ้น เจ้าควรหาก่อนว่าเสียงนั้นมาจากอะไร ไม่ควรโวยวายจนทำให้คนอื่นตกใจไปด้วย" สิงโตสอนกระต่ายด้วยความเป็นห่วง

จากนั้นสิงโตจึงนำความจริงกลับมาบอกสัตว์ทั้งหลายและแยกย้ายกันกลับไปยังถิ่นที่พักเดิมของตัวเอง

Vocabulary

1	กระต่าย	grà tàay	rabbit
2	ป่า	pàa	forest
3	สัตว์	sàt	animal
4	อาศัย	aa săi	to live
5	พักผ่อน	phák phàwn	to settle down, rest
6	ต้นมะพร้าว	tôn má phráaw	coconut tree
7	เพลิดเพลิน	phlêrrt phlerrn	contented
8	เสียงดังสนั่น	sĭang dang sà-nàn	loud thundering sound
9	น่ากลัว	nâa glua	frightening
10	แผ่นดินถล่ม	phàehn din thà lòm	landslide
11	กระโดด	grà-dòht	to leap, jump
12	ไม่เหลียวหลัง	mâi lĭaw lăng	without (so much as) a backward glance
13	ตะโกน	tà-gohn	to bellow, shout
14	วิ่งหนี	wîng nĭi	to flee
15	สิงโต	sĭng-toh	lion
16	ฝุ่นฟุ้งกระจาย	fùn fúung grà jaay	cloud of dust
17	หน้าผา	nâa phăa	cliff
18	สูงชัน	sŭung chan	steep
19	เมตตา	mêht taa	compassion
20	คำราม	kham raam	to roar
21	ภวังค์	phá wang	daydream, reverie
22	แรด	râeht	rhinoceros
23	ควาย	khwaay	buffalo
24	หมูป่า	mŭu pàa	boar
25	กวาง	gwaang	deer
26	ได้ยิน	dâi-yin	to hear

27	ข้อเท็จจริง	**khâw thét jing**	truth
28	กล้าหาญ	**glâa hăan**	fearless, brave
29	เขย่า	**khà-yào**	to shake
30	โวยวาย	**wohy-waay**	to yell, scream
31	ตกใจ	**tòk jai**	to be surprised
32	เป็นห่วง	**pen hùang**	concerned
33	แยกย้าย	**yâehk yáay**	to disperse

Culture Notes

The rabbit did not stop to consider the possible consequences of his actions in advance and made a ruckus, causing others unnecessary suffering. The rabbit acted inappropriately, and his brashness might have caused harm to others as well as his own credibility. This story is a metaphor about people who are easily frightened and who readily believe anything anyone says without due diligence.

Comprehension Questions

1. กระต่ายนอนพักผ่อนที่ไหน
2. ทำไมกระต่ายคิดว่าแผ่นดินถล่ม
3. มีสัตว์กี่ตัวที่บอกว่าเห็นแผ่นดินถล่ม มีสัตว์อะไรบ้าง
4. สิงโตทำอะไร ทำให้สัตว์ทั้งหลายหยุดวิ่ง

Writing Activity

เขียนตอนจบของเรื่องใหม่ คิดว่าจะเกิดอะไรขึ้นถ้าสิงโตไม่ทำให้สัตว์ทั้งหลาย หยุดวิ่งและตรวจสอบข้อเท็จจริง คิดว่าเรื่องนี้จะจบอย่างไร

Write a new ending to the story. Think about how the story would have ended if the lion had not stopped the other animals and had not discovered the truth.

The Crow and the Swans

There was once a crow who, despite having lustrous, ebony plumage, was not satisfied with her appearance. This made her feel insecure, so she would always do everything in her power to look better. One day, she saw a bevy of swans and marveled at their stunning white feathers and the majestic way they floated across the surface of the pond. The crow shouted, "Oh, splendid white swans, can you please tell me how I can get such beautiful white feathers? I so desire plumage such as yours! Please help me." The white swans were indifferent to the crow's pleas and merely continued searching the water for food. The crow thought that perhaps the swans had not heard her, so she called out again. But the swans showed no interest, glaring back at the crow as if profoundly annoyed.

กาในฝูงหงส์

มีกาตัวหนึ่งขนสวยดำสนิทและเงางาม แต่กลับไม่พอใจในตัวเอง เกิด
ความน้อยเนื้อต่ำใจและพยายามทำทุกวิธีเพื่อให้ตัวเองดูดีขึ้น วันหนึ่งมีฝูง
หงส์บินลงมา กาเห็นหงส์กำลังลอยตัวอยู่เหนือน้ำจึงรู้สึกชื่นชมในความ
สง่างามและขนสีขาวของหงส์มาก การ้องตะโกนออกไปว่า "ท่านหงส์ขาว
ผู้งดงาม ท่านช่วยแนะนำข้าได้ไหมว่าท่านทำอย่างไรถึงได้มีขนสีขาวที่
งดงามแบบนี้ ข้าอยากมีขนสีขาวเหมือนท่าน ช่วยบอกข้าด้วย" ส่วนหงส์
ขาวทำเป็นไม่สนใจกับคำพูดของกา ยืนอยู่กลางน้ำและหาอาหารต่อ กา
นึกว่าหงส์คงไม่ได้ยินจึงร้องถามอีกครั้ง แต่หงส์ไม่สนใจ หันมามองกา
เหมือนกับรำคาญเต็มที

Seeing that the swans were paying her no mind, the crow had an idea. She would observe the swans' every mannerism as they went about their day and try to replicate them for herself. The crow began to imitate the swans, carefully watching and mimicking their every action, morning and night, day after day. The crow refused to eat, never letting the swans out of her sight. Behaving as a swan made her feel happy. She said to them, "If I continue to act as you do, surely it will not be long before I have plumage as fair as yours." The crow figured that if she stood in the water long enough, it would turn her white like the swans.

The swans said, "Crow, do not waste your time. The day will never come when you will have feathers such as ours. We were born with this white plumage just as you were born with black. What is more, you are surely going to fall ill, as the weather here is quite cool. You should get out of the water." Then, the swans flew away.

The crow continued to go into the water every day, trying to preen as the swans did. The days turned into months and the months into years. The supply of fruit in the area began to run out, and the crow became emaciated from hunger. But her feathers still showed no sign of changing. They were just as jet-black as they always had been. Eventually, the crow lost the strength to preen in the water and was unable to fly away, so she fell ill and died.

เมื่อหงส์ขาวไม่สนใจ กาคิดวิธีบางอย่างได้คือต้องเฝ้ามองดูทุก
อิริยาบถของหงส์ว่าในแต่ละวันทำอะไรบ้าง กาก็เริ่มเลียนแบบ พยายาม
มองดูหงส์และทำตามทุกอย่างตั้งแต่เช้าจนถึงเย็นวันแล้ววันเล่า กาไม่
ยอมกินอะไรมัวแต่เฝ้ามองหงส์ไม่ให้คลาดสายตา การู้สึกดีใจที่ทำอย่าง
หงส์ได้ กาบอกกับหงส์ว่า "ท่านหงส์ข้าทำอย่างท่านได้คงใช้เวลาอีกไม่
นานก็จะมีขนสีขาวเหมือนท่านแน่นอน" กาเข้าใจว่าถ้ายืนในน้ำนาน ๆ
จะทำให้ขนขาวเหมือนกับหงส์ได้

หงส์พูดว่า "เจ้ากาอย่ามาเสียเวลาเลย เจ้าไม่มีวันจะมีขนสีขาวได้อย่าง
ข้าหรอก เพราะข้าเกิดมาก็มีขนสีขาวแบบนี้แล้ว ส่วนเจ้าก็เช่นกัน เกิดมา
มีขนสีดำ เจ้าก็ควรพอใจในสิ่งที่เจ้ามี ทำไมต้องมายืนแช่น้ำให้เหนื่อย
เปล่า แถมเจ้าอาจจะไม่สบาย อากาศที่นี่เย็นมากเจ้ารีบขึ้นมาจากน้ำเถอะ"
จากนั้นหงส์ก็บินจากไป

ตั้งแต่นั้นมากาก็ลงเล่นน้ำทุกวัน พยายามเอาปากไซ้ขนของมัน
เหมือนที่หงส์ทำ เวลาผ่านไปจากวันเป็นเดือนจากเดือนเป็นปี ผลไม้แถว
นั้นที่หากินได้ก็ร่อยหรอลงเรื่อย ๆ กาเริ่มอดอยากผอมโซ แต่ขนของมัน
ก็ยังไม่มีทีท่าว่าจะขาวขึ้นเลย ยังคงดำสนิทเหมือนเช่นเดิม ในที่สุดกาก็
หมดเรี่ยวแรงที่จะเล่นน้ำและไซ้ขน และไม่มีแรงที่จะบิน จึงค่อย ๆ ล้ม
ป่วยและอดตาย

Vocabulary

1	กา	**gaa**	crow
2	ขน	**khŏn**	plumage
3	ดำสนิท	**dam sà-nìt**	ebony, jet black
4	เงางาม	**ngao ngaam**	lustrous
5	พอใจ	**phaw jai**	satisfied
6	น้อยเนื้อต่ำใจ	**náwy núea tàm jai**	to feel insecure
7	ฝูงหงส์	**fŭung hŏng**	a bevy of swans
8	ลอยตัว	**lawy tua**	to float
9	ชื่นชม	**chûehn chom**	to marvel
10	สง่างาม	**sà-ngàa ngaam**	majestic
11	งดงาม	**ngót-ngaam**	splendid, beautiful
12	ไม่สนใจ	**mâi sŏn jai**	indifferent, uninterested, to pay (someone) no mind
13	หาอาหาร	**hăa aa hăan**	to search for food
14	รำคาญ	**ram khaan**	annoyed
15	เฝ้ามอง	**fâo mawng**	to observe
16	ได้ยิน	**dâi yin**	to hear
17	อิริยาบถ	**ì-rí-yaa-bòt**	mannerism
18	เลียนแบบ	**lian bàehp**	to mimic, imitate
19	วันแล้ววันเล่า	**wan láehw wan lâo**	day after day
20	เสียเวลา	**sĭa weh laa**	to waste time
21	ไม่สบาย	**mâi sà baay**	ill
22	อากาศ	**aa gàat**	weather
23	บิน	**bin**	to fly
24	ใช้ขน	**sái khŏn**	to preen

25	ผลไม้	**phŏn-lá-mái**	fruit
26	ร่อยหรอ	**râwy răw**	to run out
27	อดอยาก	**òt-yàak**	hunger
28	ผอมโซ	**phăwm soh**	to become emaciated
29	ตาย	**taay**	to die

Culture Notes

Crows and swans appear often in literature. Black crows are often seen as a symbol of bad luck, death, and evil. Meanwhile, swans are a symbol of purity and detachment because their feathers are white and remain so even when in the water. According to Thai belief and Buddhism that was influenced by the varna system from India, white refers to a pure and bright mind, where-as black represents violence, covetousness and impurity.

Comprehension Questions

1. ขนของกาเป็นอย่างไร
2. กาทำอะไรเพื่อทำให้ขนขาวเหมือนกับหงส์
3. กาเริ่มอดอยากผอมโซเพราะอะไร
4. เมื่อเวลาผ่านไปเป็นปีในที่สุดเกิดอะไรขึ้นกับกา

Writing Activity

เขียนอธิบายว่าคุณชอบอ่านนิทานเรื่องนี้หรือไม่ เพราะอะไร

Did you enjoy reading this story? Why or why not?

The Lizard and the Gold

There was once a lizard that lived on a king's garden gate. One day, as the king passed the gate, he saw the lizard scurry down onto the ground and then lower its head as if in a show of respect. The king asked a soldier who was guarding the gate, "Why does this lizard bow its head?" The soldier responded, "The lizard is bowing out of fealty." Hearing this pleased the king, and from then on, he provided the soldier with a piece of gold each day so that he might buy meat to feed the lizard.

One day, the soldier was unable to buy meat, as it was a holy day. Instead, he took the gold he had been given and tied it around the lizard's neck. Upon receiving the gold, the lizard became proud and thought to itself, "Henceforth, I will bow my head to no one." Some days later, the king walked past and noticed the same lizard on the gate with its head held high, no longer prostrating itself before him. The king thought this strange, and asked the soldier guarding the gate, "Tell me, why is this lizard not bowing its head as it did before?" The soldier replied, "I tied some gold around its neck, and since then, it has not bowed for anyone."

กิ้งก่าได้ทอง

กิ้งก่าตัวหนึ่งอาศัยอยู่ที่ซุ้มประตูสวนของพระราชา อยู่มาวันหนึ่งพระ
ราชาเดินผ่านซุ้มประตูเห็นกิ้งก่าคลานลงมาอยู่ที่พื้นดินแล้วผงกหัวคล้าย
คำนับ พระราชาจึงถามทหารที่เฝ้าซุ้มประตูว่า "กิ้งก่าตัวนี้ผงกหัวทำไม"
ทหารบอกว่า "เหตุที่กิ้งก่าผงกหัวเพราะมีความจงรักภักดี" พระราชาได้
ฟังแล้วก็รู้สึกพอใจจึงมอบทองคำให้ทหารที่เฝ้าซุ้มประตูไปซื้อเนื้อมาให้
กิ้งก่ากินทุกวัน

อยู่มาวันหนึ่งทหารหาซื้อเนื้อที่ตลาดไม่ได้เนื่องจากเป็นวันพระ จึงนำ
ทองคำไปผูกไว้ที่คอกิ้งก่าแทน พอกิ้งก่าได้ทองคำก็เกิดความเย่อหยิ่งคิด
ในใจว่า "ต่อไปนี้เราจะไม่ก้มหัวให้ใครอีกเด็ดขาด" วันหนึ่งพระราชามา
ถึงซุ้มประตูก็เห็นกิ้งก่าตัวเดิมชูคออยู่บนซุ้มประตูไม่คำนับเหมือนแต่
ก่อน พระราชารู้สึกแปลกใจจึงถามทหารที่เฝ้าซุ้มประตูว่า "ช่วยบอกเรา
หน่อยว่าเหตุใดกิ้งก่าตัวนี้จึงไม่ผงกหัวคำนับเหมือนแต่ก่อน" ทหารจึง
ตอบไปว่า "ข้าพเจ้าได้นำทองคำไปผูกคอให้กิ้งก่าตัวนี้ ตั้งแต่นั้นมันก็ไม่
เคยก้มหัวให้ใครเลย"

The king was disappointed and displeased with the lizard, who had become impudent, all because of some gold tied around its neck. So, he ordered the soldier to take back the gold and not buy any more meat for the lizard, under any circumstances.

Vocabulary

1	กิ้งก่า	**gîng gàa**	lizard
2	อาศัยอยู่	**aa-sǎi yùu**	to live
3	ประตู	**prà-tuu**	gate
4	สวน	**sǔan**	garden
5	พระราชา	**phrá raa chaa**	king
6	ผ่าน	**phàan**	to pass
7	พื้นดิน	**phúehn din**	ground
8	ผงกหัว	**phà-ngòk hǔa**	to lower one's head, bow
9	คำนับ	**kham náp**	a show of respect, prostration
10	ความจงรักภักดี	**khwaam jong rák phák-dii**	fealty
11	เฝ้า	**fâo**	to guard
12	ทหาร	**thá-hǎan**	soldier
13	มอบ	**mâwp**	to give, provide
14	ทองคำ	**thawng kham**	gold
15	เนื้อ	**núea**	meat
16	วันพระ	**wan phrá**	holy day
17	ผูก	**phùuk**	to tie
18	คอ	**khaw**	neck
19	เย่อหยิ่ง	**yêrr yìng**	prideful
20	ชูคอ	**chuu khaw**	with (one's) head held high

เมื่อพระราชารู้สึกผิดหวังและโกรธที่กิ้งก่าหยิ่งยโสเพราะเห็นว่าตนเอง
มีทองคำผูกคออยู่ จึงสั่งนายทหารให้เอาทองคำออกจากคอของกิ้งก่า
และไม่ต้องซื้อเนื้อมาให้กิ้งก่ากินอีกเป็นอันขาด

21	แปลกใจ	plàehk jai	strange
22	ผิดหวัง	phìt wăng	disappointed
23	โกรธ	gròht	displeased
24	ยโส	yá-sŏh	impudent
25	ไม่.....อีก	mâi...ìik	no longer, not ... anymore

Culture Notes

"The Lizard and the Gold" is a parable that warns against arrogant or haugh-
ty behavior and is often alluded to when reprimanding a person who has
lost touch with their humble beginnings. It is especially used when referring
to someone who was once of a lower social status but after gaining wealth
and power, lose themselves, abuse their power, and believe themselves to
be above others.

Comprehension Questions

1. กิ้งก่าอาศัยอยู่ที่ไหน
2. ทำไมกิ้งก่าผงกหัวให้พระราชา
3. ทหารนำทองคำไปผูกไว้ที่ไหน
4. พระราชารู้สึกอย่างไรเมื่อกิ้งก่าไม่ผงกหัวคำนับเหมือนแต่ก่อน

Writing Activity

เขียนเรียบเรียงใหม่ด้วยสำนวนของตัวเอง

Become a storyteller and rewrite this story in your own words.

The Fox and the Goat

One day, a fox stumbled into a well and, although it was not terribly deep, was not able to climb out on her own. After a long while, a thirsty goat happened to pass by and saw the fox in the well. The goat asked the fox, "How is the water in this well? Is it refreshing?"

The fox concealed her despair beneath a cheerful expression, gestured at the plentiful water, and replied, "It is the best in the country! Jump in and try some for yourself! There is more than enough for both of us!" The goat, who had long been craving a drink, did not hesitate and promptly plunged into the well. When the goat had had his fill, the fox suggested that they climb out of the well together.

สุนัขจิ้งจอกกับแพะ

วันหนึ่งมีสุนัขจิ้งจอกตกลงไปในบ่อน้ำ ถึงแม้บ่อน้ำจะไม่ลึกมาก แต่ก็
กลับขึ้นไปด้วยตัวเองไม่ได้ สักพักใหญ่ก็มีแพะตัวหนึ่งซึ่งหิวน้ำมากเดิน
ผ่านมาเห็นสุนัขจิ้งจอกในบ่อน้ำ แพะจึงถามสุนัขจิ้งจอกว่า "น้ำในบ่อน้ำ
เป็นอย่างไรบ้าง สดชื่นไหม"

สุนัขจิ้งจอกปกปิดความเศร้าไว้ภายใต้ใบหน้าที่ร่าเริงสนุกสนาน มัน
ทำท่าให้ดูว่ามีน้ำอย่างเหลือล้น และตอบกลับไปว่า "ดีที่สุดในประเทศนี้
เลย ลองกระโดดลงมากินดูสิ มีน้ำมากพอสำหรับเราทั้งคู่เลย" แพะซึ่งหิว
น้ำมากเป็นทุนเดิมอยู่แล้ว จึงไม่ลังเลรีบกระโดดลงไปในบ่อน้ำทันที จน
เมื่อแพะได้กินน้ำเรียบร้อยแล้วนั้น สุนัขจิ้งจอกจึงบอกแพะว่า "เราจะขึ้น
ไปจากบ่อน้ำพร้อมกัน"

The fox explained the plan. "You must plant your front legs against the wall of the well, and then I will run up your back and jump out. After that, I will help you up." The goat agreed, readily trusting the fox. The fox clambered atop the goat's back and climbed easily onto the rim of the well but then swiftly vanished.

The goat realized that he had been tricked into becoming the fox's escape ladder. He cursed the fox who had broken her promise. Not long thereafter, the fox returned once again. The goat pleaded for her to pull him out of the well. But the fox only mocked him, saying, "I'm leaving, you foolish goat. If you have as much brain as you do beard, you will not dive into a well without first looking for a way out and not land yourself in peril from which you cannot escape." With this, the fox sauntered off and disappeared into the woods.

สุนัขจิ้งจอกบรรยายแผนว่า "แพะต้องเอาขาหน้ายึดไว้ที่ผนังบ่อและก้ม หัวลง ข้าจะวิ่งขึ้นไปบนหลังเจ้าและออกไปได้ แล้วข้าก็จะช่วยเจ้าขึ้นไป" แพะก็เชื่ออย่างง่ายดาย หลังจากนั้นสุนัขจิ้งจอกก็กระโดดขึ้นบนหลังแพะ แล้วปีนขึ้นไปยังขอบบ่อได้อย่างสบาย แต่กลับหนีหายไปอย่างเร็ว

เมื่อรู้ตัวว่าถูกหลอกใช้เป็นบันไดเพื่อให้สุนัขจิ้งจอกปีนออกไปได้ แพะ ร้องประณามสุนัขจิ้งจอกที่ไม่ทำตามสัญญา ไม่นานสุนัขจิ้งจอกก็หวน กลับมาอีกครั้ง แพะจึงขอร้องให้สุนัขจิ้งจอกช่วยดึงมันขึ้นไปด้วย แต่สุนัข จิ้งจอกพูดเยาะเย้ยว่า "ลาก่อนนะเจ้าแพะหน้าโง่ ถ้าเจ้ามีมันสมองเยอะ เหมือนเคราของเจ้า เจ้าคงไม่ลงไปในบ่อโดยที่ไม่ดูว่าจะขึ้นมาได้หรือเปล่า และคงไม่พาตัวเองไปอยู่ในที่มีภัยซึ่งเจ้าไม่มีทางจะหลบหนีออกมาได้" แล้วสุนัขจิ้งจอกก็เดินหายเข้าไปในป่า

Vocabulary

1	สุนัขจิ้งจอก	sù nák jîng jàwk	fox
2	ตก	tòk	to stumble, fall
3	บ่อน้ำ	bàw náam	well
4	ลึก	lúek	deep
5	สักพัก	sàk phák	a while
6	แพะ	pháe	goat
7	หิวน้ำ	hǐw náam	thirsty
8	สดชื่น	sòt chûehn	refreshing
9	ปกปิด	pòk pìt	to conceal
10	ความเศร้า	khwaam sâo	despair
11	ร่าเริง, สนุกสนาน	râa rerrng, sà nùk sà năan	cheerful
12	ทำท่า	tham thâa	to act, gesture
13	เหลือล้น	lŭea lón	plentiful
14	ดีที่สุด	dii thîi sùt	the best
15	ประเทศ	prà têht	country
16	ลังเล	lang leh	to hesitate
17	พร้อมกัน	phrâwm gan	together
18	แผน	phăehn	plan
19	ขาหน้า	khăa nâa	front legs
20	ผนัง	phà-năng	wall
21	ปีน	piin	to climb, clamber
22	เชื่อ	chûea	to trust
23	หายไป	hăay pai	to vanish
24	ถูกหลอก	thùuk làwk	to be tricked
25	บันได	ban-dai	ladder

26	ประณาม	**prà-naam**	to curse
27	สัญญา	**săn-yaa**	promise
28	สมอง	**sà-măwng**	brain
29	เครา	**khrao**	beard
30	เยาะเย้ย	**yáw-yéhy**	to mock

Culture Notes

This fable teaches that any action not taken with caution might lead to suffering. Before any decision or action is taken, we should think through our methods first. If not, we might regret it later—just like the goat who jumped into the well to quench his thirst without considering how he would get out.

Comprehension Questions

1. สุนัขจิ้งจอกตกลงไปที่ไหน
2. สุนัขจิ้งจอกทำอย่างไรจึงปีนออกไปได้
3. ทำไมแพะไม่ลังเลรีบกระโดดลงไปในบ่อน้ำทันที
4. สุนัขจิ้งจอกเปรียบสมองของแพะเหมือนกับอะไร

Writing Activity

เขียนอธิบายว่าคุณอยากเป็นใครในนิทานเรื่องนี้ เพราะอะไร

Imagine you were part of this story. Explain which character you would like to be and why.

The Blind Hen

A long time ago, there was a village whose inhabitants grew an assortment of crops such as rice, cassava, corn, sugarcane, and fruit. Bun Chuay was a farmer who grew fruit trees and planted vegetables. On top of that, he looked after two hens and a rooster. One of the hens had normal eyesight, and the other was blind.

Every morning, the blind hen would wake up at dawn to scratch at the ground in front of her coop, diligently combing the soil for bits of food. The sighted hen, by contrast, never strayed far after waking up in the morning, for fear of her feathers becoming dirty and her soft feet becoming coarse and caked with mud.

The sighted hen lived a cozy life, pecking lazily at the vegetables and fruit that the blind hen provided. While helping to raise the hens, Bun Chuay saw the sighted hen's behavior and could only shake his head in exasperation. He said, "The hen with good eyes has the blind hen going out in search of food. I cannot bear raising such an ill-mannered animal." Having said this, Bun Chuay angrily chased the sighted hen out of the coop.

The sighted hen had been so proud of her soft feet and sleek feathers but was of no use to herself or anyone else. She could not fend for herself, as she had only known a life in which others had looked after her.

แม่ไก่ตาบอด

นานมาแล้วที่หมู่บ้านแห่งหนึ่งชาวบ้านทำเกษตรผสมผสาน คือ ปลูกข้าว
มันสำปะหลัง ข้าวโพด อ้อย หรือผลไม้ บุญช่วยเป็นชาวสวน เขาปลูก
ผลไม้และผักนานาชนิด นอกจากนี้เขายังเลี้ยงแม่ไก่ไว้สองตัวกับพ่อไก่
หนึ่งตัว แต่แม่ไก่ที่เลี้ยงไว้มีตัวหนึ่งตาดี ส่วนอีกตัวหนึ่งตาบอด

ตอนเช้าทุกวันแม่ไก่ตาบอดจะตื่นแต่เช้าออกไปคุ้ยเขี่ยพื้นดินหน้าบ้าน
เพื่อหาอาหารกินอย่างขยันขันแข็ง ส่วนแม่ไก่ตาดีนั้น เมื่อตื่นขึ้นมาไม่
เคยไปไหนไกลเพราะกลัวว่าขนจะเลอะฝุ่นและเท้าที่อ่อนนุ่มทั้งสองข้างจะ
หยาบกร้านและเปื้อนดินโคลน

แม่ไก่ตาดีใช้ชีวิตอย่างสุขสบาย คอยจิกกินผักผลไม้ที่แม่ไก่ตาบอดหา
มาให้ บุญช่วยผู้เป็นเจ้าของไก่ทั้งสองตัวเห็นพฤติกรรมของแม่ไก่ตาดีแล้ว
ก็ได้แต่ส่ายหัวด้วยความเอือมระอา แล้วพูดว่า "เป็นไก่ตาดีมองเห็น
ชัดเจนกลับให้ไก่ตาบอดต้องหาอาหารมาให้ นิสัยแบบนี้สงสัยจะเลี้ยงไว้
ไม่ได้แล้ว" ว่าแล้วบุญช่วยก็ไล่แม่ไก่ตาดีออกจากบ้านไปด้วยความโมโห

แม่ไก่ตาดีที่มักภูมิใจกับเท้าที่อ่อนนุ่มขนสวยงาม แต่ต้องมีชีวิตอยู่ไป
วัน ๆ โดยไม่มีประโยชน์กับตัวเองและผู้อื่นเลย เพราะไม่สามารถหาเลี้ยง
ตัวเองได้ คอยแต่อาศัยให้ผู้อื่นหาเลี้ยง

Vocabulary

1	หมู่บ้าน	**mùu bâan**	village
2	ชาวบ้าน	**chaaw bâan**	villager
3	เกษตรผสมผสาน	**gà sèht phà sŏm phà săan**	growing a variety of crops
4	ปลูก	**plùuk**	to grow
5	ข้าว	**khâaw**	rice
6	มันสำปะหลัง	**man săm pà lăng**	cassava
7	ข้าวโพด	**khâaw phôht**	corn
8	อ้อย	**âwy**	sugarcane
9	ผลไม้	**phŏn lá máai**	fruit
10	ชาวสวน	**chaaw sŭan**	farmer
11	ผัก	**phàk**	vegetable
12	เลี้ยง	**líang**	to raise, look after
13	แม่ไก่	**mâeh gài**	hen
14	ตาดี	**taa dii**	good eyesight
15	ตาบอด	**taa bàwt**	blind
16	ตอนเช้า	**tawn cháo**	morning
17	ตื่น	**tùehn**	to wake up
18	คุ้ยเขี่ย	**khúy khìa**	to scratch
19	ขยัน	**khà yăn**	diligent
20	หาอาหาร	**hăa aa-hăan**	to search for food
21	ไกล	**glai**	far
22	กลัว	**glua**	to fear
23	เลอะฝุ่น	**lér fùn**	to become dirty
24	หยาบกร้าน	**yàap grâan**	coarse

25	พฤติกรรม	**phrúet-tì-gam**	behavior
26	เอือมระอา	**ueam-rá-aa**	exasperation
27	นิสัย	**ní-sǎi**	manners
28	หาเลี้ยง	**hǎa-líang**	to fend for, look after

Culture Notes

This fable is similar to the Thai proverb "**yàa ngaw mueh ngaw tháo**," which means that we must know how to take care of ourselves, regardless of our physical condition, even if we have a disability. If we work hard we might even be more valuable than able-bodied people who do not know how to provide for themselves.

Comprehension Questions

1. ชาวบ้านทำเกษตรผสมผสานปลูกอะไรบ้าง
2. บุญช่วยเลี้ยงพ่อไก่กับแม่ไก่กี่ตัว
3. ทำไมแม่ไก่ตาดีไม่คุ้ยเขี่ยดินเพื่อหาอาหาร
4. เมื่อแม่ไก่ตาดีออกจากบ้าน มีชีวิตอย่างไร

Writing Activity

เลือกคำใหม่หรือคำที่น่าสนใจ 10 คำจากนิทาน และเขียนประโยคใหม่จากคำ
ที่เลือก

Choose ten interesting or new words from this story and write a new sentence with each one.

The Rich Man and the Gold

On the outskirts of a town lived a rich, miserly man named Maana. He worked diligently without rest to earn his living, seven days a week, year after year. Whenever Maana was able to turn a profit, he would use the money to buy bars of gold, which he would then bury in the ground. This is because Maana thought that if he stored his gold inside his house, it would be possible for a thief to break in and steal it.

เศรษฐีกับทองคำ

แถวชานเมืองมีเศรษฐีขี้เหนียวคนหนึ่งชื่อ "มานะ" เขาเป็นคนขยันทำมา
หากินและไม่เคยหยุดพักสักวัน เขาทำงานทั้งเจ็ดวันในหนึ่งสัปดาห์ ทำ
แบบนี้ปีแล้วปีเล่า เมื่อมานะได้กำไรได้เงินมา เขาก็นำเงินไปซื้อทองคำ
แท่งแล้วนำไปฝังไว้ใต้ดิน เพราะมานะคิดว่าหากเก็บไว้ในบ้านอาจมีโจรมา
ขโมยทองของเขาก็เป็นได้

Maana buried the gold bars in the garden behind his house. Every day after he closed up shop, he would exhume his gold to make sure it was all still there. Unbeknownst to Maana, someone had seen him doing this. The thief, Samai, who would often burgle homes in the area, happened to spy Maana burying his gold one evening. Samai tried to stay perfectly quiet and contain the excitement he felt at seeing the gold piled there before his eyes. He waited until Maana had once again covered the hole, and then he slunk away.

Late that night, once Maana had retired for the evening, Samai tiptoed into the garden, dug up the gold, and made off with every last bar. The next evening, Maana went to exhume his gold as usual but was stunned to find that the gold bars had vanished, with only stones in their place. Dejected, Maana confided to a friend about what had happened. His friend asked, "When your gold was buried, was it being put to any use?" Maana replied, "No, I would just bury it and then dig it up every day to look at it." His friend then reasoned, "If that is the case, then you should just think of those stones as gold. You were getting no use out of the gold you had buried. You merely dug it up to admire it and then buried it again. Something of value that goes unused is no different than something of no value at all."

มานะเอาทองแท่งไปฝังไว้ในสวนหลังบ้าน ทุกวันเมื่อเขาค้าขายเสร็จ
แล้ว เขาจะมาขุดดูว่าทองคำยังอยู่ครบหรือไม่ ในระหว่างนั้นเขาไม่รู้เลยว่า
มีใครมาเห็นเข้าโดยบังเอิญ มีโจรชื่อ "สมัย" ที่ชอบลักเล็กขโมยน้อยตาม
บ้านเรือนแอบมาเห็นมานะขุดทองคำในตอนเย็นนั้นพอดี สมัยพยายาม
นิ่งเงียบที่สุดที่จะไม่แสดงความตื่นเต้นที่เห็นทองคำอยู่ตรงหน้า แล้วก็รอ
ให้มานะฝังกลบเหมือนเดิมแล้วจากไป

ช่วงดึกของคืนนั้นสมัยเห็นว่ามานะน่าจะนอนหลับแล้ว จึงแอบย่องมา
ขุดทองคำไปจนหมด ตอนเย็นวันรุ่งขึ้นมานะก็มาขุดดูทองตามปกติ แต่
ต้องตกใจมากเพราะทองคำที่ฝังไว้ทั้งหมดหายไป พบเพียงก้อนหินมาอยู่
แทนที่ทองคำ มานะเสียใจมากและไปเล่าให้เพื่อนฟัง เพื่อนจึงถามเขาว่า
"เมื่อท่านฝังทองคำพวกนั้นแล้ว ท่านได้นำทองคำไปใช้ประโยชน์บ้างหรือ
เปล่า" มานะตอบว่า "เปล่า ข้านำไปฝังไว้เฉย ๆ แล้วข้าก็มาขุดขึ้นมาดู
ทุกวัน" เพื่อนของเขาจึงแนะนำว่า "ถ้าเช่นนั้นท่านก็คิดเสียว่าก้อนหิน
พวกนี้เป็นทองคำ เพราะถึงยังไงท่านก็ไม่ใช้ประโยชน์จากทองคำที่ฝังไว้
แค่ขุดแล้วหยิบมาดูชื่นชม แล้วก็ฝังกลบไว้เหมือนเดิม ของมีค่าที่ไม่ได้นำ
มาใช้ ย่อมไม่ต่างอะไรจากของที่ไม่มีค่า"

Vocabulary

1	เศรษฐี	**sèht thǐi**	rich man
2	ชานเมือง	**chaan mueang**	outskirts of town
3	ขี้เหนียว	**khîi nǐaw**	miserly
4	ทำมาหากิน	**tham maa hǎa gin**	to earn a living
5	ทำงาน	**tham ngaan**	to work
6	สัปดาห์	**sàp daa**	week
7	กำไร	**gam rai**	profit
8	เงิน	**ngerrn**	money
9	ซื้อ	**súeh**	to buy
10	ทองคำแท่ง	**thawng kham thâehng**	bricks/bars of gold
11	ฝัง	**fǎng**	to bury
12	ใต้ดิน	**tâi din**	in the ground
13	เก็บ	**gèp**	to store
14	โจร	**john**	thief
15	ขโมย	**khà-mohy**	to steal
16	สวนหลังบ้าน	**sǔan lǎng bâan**	backyard garden
17	ขุด	**khùt**	to exhume, dig up
18	บังเอิญ	**bang-errn**	to happen to..., by coincidence
19	ลักเล็กขโมยน้อย	**lák lék khà-mohy náwy**	to burgle
20	นิ่งเงียบ	**nîng ngîap**	to be/stay quiet
21	ความตื่นเต้น	**khwaam tùehn têhn**	excitement
22	ฝังกลบ	**fǎng gròp**	to bury, cover a hole
23	ดึก	**dùek**	late at night
24	นอนหลับ	**nawn làp**	to retire (go to bed)

25	ย่อง	yâwng	to tiptoe
26	หายไป	hăay pai	to vanish
27	ก้อนหิน	gâwn hĭn	stone
28	ใช้ประโยชน์	chái prà yòht	to put (something) to use
29	ชื่นชม	chûehn chom	to admire
30	มีค่า	mii khâa	of value

Culture Notes

This fable teaches that valuable things that are not used will end up being useless. It has the same meaning as the Thai proverb "**gài dâi ploy**" (similar to the English proverb "pearls before swine"), which is often used to refer to someone who owns something valuable but does not understand its value or know how to use it to their advantage—in effect, rendering it useless.

Comprehension Questions

1. มานะเป็นคนขยัน เขาทำงานกี่วันในหนึ่งสัปดาห์
2. มานะฝังทองคำแท่งไว้ที่ไหน
3. เมื่อแอบเห็นมานะขุดทองคำ โจรชื่อสมัยทำอะไร
4. มานะพบอะไรมาอยู่แทนที่ทองคำที่ฝังไว้แล้วหายไป

Writing Activity

เขียนเล่าว่าเกิดอะไรขึ้นกับมานะหลังจากทองคำที่ฝังไว้แล้วหายไป

Write about what might have happened to Maana after his gold bars were stolen.

The Horse-Faced Woman

In the City of Mithila, there was a girl named Kaew, who had a face not un-like that of a horse. Anyone who saw her would mock her appearance. But her mother would console her, saying that beauty was not on one's face but in one's heart and that if Kaew was persistent in doing good, then others would see that beauty. Her equine appearance prompted the villagers to call her "horse-faced Kaew."

The city was ruled by King Phuwadon and Queen Nantha, whose son was named Pin Thong. One day, Prince Pin Thong had traveled out of the palace to fly his kite near the village. Suddenly a gust of wind arose, yanking the string from his hand and setting the kite far adrift. It was Kaew who retrieved the lost kite, and she was going to keep it for herself. But Prince Pin Thong had followed after it and requested its return. Kaew consented on the condition that the prince promise to take her into the palace as his consort. This infuriated the prince, who thought this woman quite irritating, indeed. But he acquiesced for the sole reason that he desperately wanted his kite returned to him. Kaew waited many days, but Pin Thong

แก้วหน้าม้า

เมืองมิถิลามีหญิงสาวหน้าตาคล้ายม้า ชื่อ "แก้ว" ใครเห็นก็พากันหัวเราะ
ที่แก้วมีหน้าเป็นม้า แม่ปลอบแก้วว่าความสวยงามไม่ได้อยู่ที่หน้าตา แต่
อยู่ที่จิตใจมากกว่า ถ้าแก้วหมั่นทำความดี ทุกคนจะเห็นความงามของแก้ว
เนื่องจากใบหน้าเหมือนม้า ชาวบ้านจึงเรียกแก้วว่า "แก้วหน้าม้า"

ในเมืองนี้มีท้าวภูวดลกับพระนางนันทาปกครองเมืองและมีลูกชายชื่อ
"ปิ่นทอง" วันหนึ่งพระปิ่นทองออกไปเล่นว่าวนอกวังใกล้ ๆ กับหมู่บ้าน
ขณะที่กำลังเล่นว่าว เกิดมีลมแรงทำให้ว่าวหลุดมือและปลิวไปไกล ซึ่ง
แก้วเก็บว่าวได้และคิดว่าจะเก็บไว้เล่นเอง แต่พระปิ่นทองตามมาขอว่าว
คืน แก้วขอสัญญาจากพระปิ่นทองว่าต้องมารับเข้าวังไปเป็นมเหสี
พระปิ่นได้ยินแก้วพูดก็โกรธมากและคิดว่าหญิงคนนี้น่ารำคาญ แต่ก็
รับปากเพียงเพราะหวังอยากได้ว่าวคืน แก้วรออยู่หลายวันไม่เห็นพระปิ่น
ทองมารับ แก้วจึงเล่าเรื่องให้พ่อกับแม่ฟังและขอให้ไปทวงสัญญา เมื่อพ่อ

did not return for her. So, she told her father and mother about what had happened and requested that they go to the palace and demand that the prince keep his promise. When they told the king about the agreement Pin Thong had made with their daughter, he became enraged and summoned the prince for interrogation. Pin Thong admitted to promising Kaew that she could come live at the palace as his consort, and the queen ordered him to fulfill his obligation and to fetch the girl immediately.

When Kaew arrived at the palace, King Phuwadon and Prince Pin Thong were so repulsed by her appearance that they were unable to muster the slightest bit of civility. They soon hatched a plan to cast her out. They ordered her to bring Mount Sumeru to the village within seven days. Should she fail, she would be put to death. However, if she succeeded, she would be allowed to marry the prince.

Kaew went into the forest and prayed that she become the prince's true love and that she succeed in her quest to find Mount Sumeru. She had been traveling for three days, when she encountered a hoard of fierce animals. They were just about to attack when a hermit appeared and came to her aid. The hermit took pity on Kaew and removed her horse face, turning her into a beautiful woman named Kaew Mani. He then summoned a flying ship and a magnificent dagger for her to use as a weapon. Kaew took leave of the hermit, once again donning her horse face. She used the ship to fly to Mount Sumeru, which she brought back with her to the palace and presented to the king.

In an attempt to avoid fulfilling his obligation, the king schemed to have the prince travel to another city. Before leaving, Pin Thong said that if, upon his return, Kaew had not borne him a child she would be executed. Kaew soon concocted a plan and hurried out of the palace to lie in wait for her prince on his journey back home. She removed her horse face and transformed herself into Kaew Mani. She then asked to stay with an elderly couple who lived in the forest. When the prince eventually passed by, she pretended to be bathing in a nearby stream. Pin Thong saw her and fell instantly in love. He courted her, and eventually they moved in together. When Kaew Mani became pregnant, the prince bestowed upon her a ring to give to the unborn child, which would prove their true parentage.

แม่ไปทวงสัญญากับพระปิ่นทอง ท้าวภูวดลโกรธให้เรียกลูกชายมาสอบ
ถาม พระปิ่นทองยอมรับว่าสัญญาจะให้มาอยู่ เมื่อพระปิ่นทองสัญญาแล้ว
พระนางนันทาสั่งให้ไปรับตัวแก้วมาอยู่ในวัง

พอมาถึงวังหลวง ท้าวภูวดลกับพระปิ่นทองเห็นแก้วรูปร่างหน้าตาน่า
เกลียดและกิริยามารยาทกระโดดกระเดกก็ทนไม่ได้ แก้วเข้าวังมาไม่นาน
ท้าวภูวดลกับพระปิ่นทองก็หาทางกำจัดแก้ว โดยสั่งให้นางแก้วไปยกเขา
พระสุเมรุมาไว้ในเมืองภายใน 7 วัน หากทำไม่สำเร็จจะต้องได้รับโทษ
ประหาร แต่ถ้าทำได้จะจัดพิธีแต่งงานกับพระปิ่นทอง

แก้วออกไปตามป่าแล้วอธิษฐานว่าหากตนเป็นเนื้อคู่ของพระปิ่นทอง
ขอให้พบเขาพระสุเมรุ แก้วเดินทางต่อไปอีกสามวันไปเจอสัตว์ร้ายในป่าที่
จ้องจะมาทำร้าย แต่มีฤาษีมาช่วยไว้ พระฤาษีมีใจเมตตาช่วยถอดหน้าม้า
ออกให้ แก้วจึงกลายเป็นหญิงที่งดงาม ชื่อว่า "นางแก้วมณี" พร้อมเสก
เรือเหาะและมีดอีโต้วิเศษให้เป็นอาวุธ แก้วกราบลาพระฤาษีพร้อมสวม
หน้าม้าดังเดิม นั่งเรือเหาะไปจนเจอเขาพระสุเมรุ แก้วจึงยกเขาพระสุเมรุ
มาให้ท้าวภูวดลได้สำเร็จ

ส่วนท้าวภูวดลพยายามหาทางที่จะเลี่ยงคำสัญญาที่มีต่อแก้ว จึงออก
อุบายให้พระปิ่นทองไปต่างเมือง ก่อนเดินทางไปพระปิ่นทองบอกว่า ถ้า
กลับมาแล้วแก้วยังไม่มีลูกจะถูกประหาร แก้วคิดหาวิธีมีลูกกับพระปิ่น
ทองได้แล้ว จึงรีบออกนอกวังไปดักรอพระปิ่นทองระหว่างทาง แก้วถอด
หน้าม้าออกเป็นนางแก้วมณี แล้วไปขออาศัยอยู่กับสองตายายในป่า เมื่อ
พระปิ่นทองผ่านมา แก้วจึงแกล้งไปอาบน้ำบริเวณนั้น จนพระปิ่นทอง
เห็นและหลงรักนางแก้วมณี และพยายามตามหานางแก้วมณีจนพบและ
ได้อยู่กินด้วยกันจนนางแก้วมณีเริ่มตั้งครรภ์ พระปิ่นทองจึงมอบแหวนไว้
ให้ลูกเพื่อยืนยันว่าเป็นลูกของพระปิ่นทองจริง

Kaew later gave birth to her son. Before returning with the infant to the palace, she once more went to visit the hermit. The hermit told Kaew that Prince Pin Thong was in danger. On his way back to the palace, he had been caught in a storm and had accidentally wandered into the domain of the ogres. So, Kaew left her child with the hermit and transformed into a man. The male Kaew then boarded the flying ship to do battle with King Phanrat, the ruler of the city of the ogres. After defeating the ogre king, Kaew allowed Pin Thong to rule over the city, asking only for the ogre king's two daughters, Soi Suwan and Chantha, to take as wives. Kaew brought them to the hermit and revealed her true form, making them vow to keep her secret and then went to present them to Pin Thong.

After spending some time in the city of the ogres, Pin Thong took Soi Suwan and Chantha back to Mithila. He was astonished to encounter Kaew and her son. At first, he did not believe that the infant was his. Then he saw the ring around the boy's wrist that he, himself, had bequeathed to him, and bestowed upon his new son the name "Pin Kaew."

King Pra Kaimat was the ogre who ruled over the city of Kraichak and was a relative of King Phanrat, whom Kaew had killed. Angered by the death of his kin, he led an attack on Mithila City. Prince Pin Thong was unskilled in battle, and Soi Suwan and Chantha were afraid he would suffer defeat at the hands of the ogre. So, they told him of Kaew's true identity so that he could seek her assistance. Out of concern for the city, Kaew agreed to assume male form and meet the ogre on the battlefield at once. But Kaew's attacks were of no use against King Pra Kaimat, as he had the power to heal his wounds. So Kaew flew his ship over the ogre's head, causing King Pra Kaimat's magic to fail, and allowing him to strike a killing blow.

Having defeated the ogre, he quickly disappeared. Prince Pin Thong was certain that the man who had helped him had been Kaew. So, he went to find her in an attempt to make amends. Kaew held out until the prince acted as though he would slit his own throat and die. She then relented and removed her horse face, to everyone's delight. The king and queen held a joyous wedding for the couple and appointed Kaew as Pin Thong's queen, giving her a new name, Mani Ratana. Not long thereafter, Kaew was once again with child, and they all lived together happily from then on.

ทางด้านแก้วได้คลอดลูกชายและคิดจะพาลูกกลับไปหาพระปิ่นทองจึง
ได้แวะไปลาพระฤาษี พระฤาษีบอกแก้วว่า พระปิ่นทองอยู่ในอันตราย
ระหว่างพระปิ่นทองเดินทางกลับวัง โดนพายุพัดเข้าไปอยู่เขตแดนของเหล่า
ยักษ์ร้าย แก้วจึงฝากลูกไว้กับพระฤาษีแล้วแปลงร่างเป็นผู้ชายขึ้นเรือเหาะ
ไปรบกับท้าวพาลราชเจ้าเมืองยักษ์จนได้รับชัยชนะ แก้วในร่างชายหนุ่ม
ยกให้พระปิ่นทองครองเมืองยักษ์ และแก้วขอเพียง" นางสร้อยสุวรรณ"
และ "นางจันทา" ลูกสาวของยักษ์ทั้งสองไปเป็นชายา แก้วพาสองสาวมา
หาฤาษีและบอกเรื่องราวที่แท้จริงว่าตนเป็นใคร และสัญญาว่าจะเก็บเป็น
ความลับ แก้วจึงพาลูกสาวทั้งสองของยักษ์มามอบให้พระปิ่นทอง

หลังจากอยู่ในเมืองยักษ์มาระยะหนึ่ง พระปิ่นทองก็พาสร้อยสุวรรณ
และจันทากลับไปยังเมืองมิถิลา และต้องประหลาดใจเมื่อได้เผชิญหน้ากับ
แก้วและลูกชาย แรกทีเดียวพระปิ่นทองไม่เชื่อว่าเด็กคนนี้เป็นลูกชาย แต่
แหวนที่ข้อมือของเด็กน้อยทำให้เขาต้องเชื่อและยอมรับว่าเป็นลูก แล้วยัง
ตั้งชื่อให้ว่า "ปิ่นแก้ว"

ทางด้าน"ท้าวประกายมาต" ยักษ์ผู้ครองเมืองไกรจักรเป็นญาติของ
ท้าวพาลราชซึ่งถูกแก้วฆ่าตายเกิดแค้นใจยกทัพมาที่เมืองมิถิลา พระปิ่น
ทองไม่ชำนาญการรบ นางสร้อยสุวรรณและนางจันทากลัวว่าพระปิ่นทอง
จะพ่ายแพ้ยักษ์ จึงบอกความจริงว่าแก้วคือใคร ให้พระปิ่นทองไปขอความ
ช่วยเหลือจากแก้ว แก้วเป็นห่วงบ้านเมืองจึงยอมช่วยโดยแปลงกายเป็น
ชายออกสู้กับยักษ์ทันที แก้วไม่สามารถทำอะไรท้าวประกายมาตได้
เพราะท้าวประกายมาตมีฤทธิ์รักษาแผลได้ แก้วจึงขี่เรือเหาะข้ามหัวท้าว
ประกายมาต ทำให้มนต์เสื่อมและฆ่าท้าวประกายมาตได้สำเร็จ

เมื่อชนะศึกแก้วในร่างของชายหนุ่มขอลากลับทันที พระปิ่นทองมั่นใจ
ว่าต้องเป็นแก้วแน่นอน จึงตามไปงอนง้อ แต่แก้วก็ยังเล่นตัวจนพระปิ่น
ทองทำทีจะเชือดคอตาย แก้วจึงยอมใจอ่อนถอดหน้าม้าออก สร้างความ
ยินดีให้กับทุกคน ท้าวภูวดลและนางนันทาจึงจัดพิธีแต่งงานอย่าง
เอิกเกริกและแต่งตั้งให้แก้วเป็นมเหสีของปิ่นทอง พร้อมกับได้ชื่อใหม่ว่า
"มณีรัตนา" ต่อมาแก้วก็ตั้งครรภ์อีกครั้งและได้อยู่ร่วมกันอย่างมีความสุข

Vocabulary

1	ปกครอง	**pòk khrawng**	to rule
2	สัญญา	**săn-yaa**	to promise
3	มเหสี	**má-hĕh-sĭi**	consort
4	วัง	**wang**	palace
5	กิริยามารยาท	**gì-rí-yaa maa rá yâat**	civility
6	ทนไม่ได้	**thon mâi dâi**	to be unable to bear (something)
7	กำจัด	**gam jàt**	to get rid of, cast out
8	โทษประหาร	**thôht prà-hăn**	to put to death
9	อธิษฐาน	**à-thít-thăan**	to pray
10	เนื้อคู่	**núea khûu**	true love
11	สัตว์ร้าย	**sàt ráay**	fierce animal
12	ฤาษี	**rueh sĭi**	hermit
13	เสก	**sèhk**	to summon
14	เรือเหาะ	**ruea hàw**	flying ship
15	มีดอีโต้	**mîit ii-tôh**	dagger
16	วิเศษ	**wí sèht**	magnificent
17	เลี่ยง	**lîang**	to avoid
18	ตั้งครรภ์	**tâng khan**	to become pregnant
19	แหวน	**wăehn**	ring
20	อันตราย	**an-tà-raay**	danger
21	ยักษ์	**yák**	ogre
22	แปลงร่าง	**plaehng râang**	to transform
23	สู้, รบ	**sûu, róp**	to do battle
24	มนต์	**mon**	magic
25	เสื่อม	**sùeam**	to fail

26	งอนง้อ	ngawn ngáw	to make amends (with someone)
27	เอิกเกริก	èrrk gà rèrrk	joyous
28	แต่งตั้ง	tàehng tâng	to appoint

Culture Notes

A Thai hermit sage is a person with the gift of clairvoyance who renounces personal pleasures, seeks solitude, and lives in seclusion in a hermitage, located in a forest or cave or on a cliff or mountain. Hermits have powers such as the ability to make themselves appear and disappear, pass through obstacles, hover in the air, and reach the moon, sun, and Brahmaloka (the highest worlds in Buddhist cosmology, consisting of 20 heavens). Thai people are very familiar with hermits, especially through various cultural traditions and works of literature. Sons of kings, for example, are required to study with hermits. In addition, textbooks in subjects such as music, dramatic arts, and traditional medicine depict the worship of hermits.

Comprehension Questions

1. ทำไมชาวบ้านจึงเรียกแก้วว่า "นางแก้วหน้าม้า"
2. ใครช่วยถอดหน้าม้าและทำให้แก้วกลายเป็นหญิงที่งดงาม
3. แก้วทำอะไรเพื่อทำให้มนต์เสื่อม และฆ่าท้าวประกายมาตได้สำเร็จ

Writing Activity

เขียนอธิบายสิ่งที่น่าสนใจ 3 อย่าง ที่เรียนรู้จากนิทานเรื่องนี้

Write about three interesting things you have learned from this story.

Krai Thong: The Crocodile Hunter

There was once a sacred underwater cave where a group of crocodiles lived. The expansive cave was divided into many rooms, large and small, and it housed a magical crystal ball that illuminated the caverns, making them as bright as day at all times. The crocodiles that entered the cave would change into humans, who never hungered nor desired food.

Residing within the cave was the ancient crocodile king Ramphai. Ramphai was pious and had long refused to eat any living thing. He had a grandson named Chalawan, who ruled over the holy cave in his grandfather's stead. However, Chalawan had a nasty habit of leaving the cave for the surface in order to capture and eat humans. This caused the villagers in the nearby city of Phichit to live in constant terror, as Chalawan was an extremely large crocodile.

ไกรทอง

มีถ้ำศักดิ์สิทธิ์แห่งหนึ่งใต้น้ำเป็นที่อาศัยของเหล่าจระเข้ทั้งหลาย ภาย
ในถ้ำกว้างใหญ่ แยกเป็นห้องใหญ่ห้องเล็กมากมาย และมีลูกแก้ววิเศษที่
ส่องแสงออกมาทำให้ในถ้ำสว่างเหมือนเวลากลางวันตลอดเวลา จระเข้ที่
เข้ามาในถ้ำก็จะกลายร่างเป็นมนุษย์ไม่มีความหิวหรืออยากกินอาหารใด ๆ
   ในถ้ำมีพญาจระเข้ผู้เฒ่าชื่อ ท้าวรำไพ เป็นราชาแห่งจระเข้ที่ไม่ยอมกิน
สิ่งมีชีวิตและบำเพ็ญตนถือศีลมาเป็นเวลานาน พญาจระเข้มีหลานชื่อ ชา
ละวัน ซึ่งได้ปกครองถ้ำศักดิ์สิทธิ์แทนปู่และพ่อ แต่ชาละวันมีนิสัย
อันธพาลชอบออกจากถ้ำขึ้นสู่ผิวน้ำจับคนกินเป็นอาหาร ทำให้ชาวบ้าน
เมืองพิจิตรกลัวกันมาก เพราะเป็นจระเข้ที่ใหญ่โตมาก

One day, after leaving the cave, Chalawan encountered two girls, named Taphao Kaew and Taphao Thong, swimming in the river. The girls were sisters and the daughters of the ruler of Phichit City. Chalawan was captivated by Taphao Thong's beauty and snatched her up his jaws, dragging her down into the cave. Once inside the cave, Chalawan changed into a handsome young man. Taphao Thong later regained consciousness and was awestruck by the cavern's grandeur. Chalawan came to her in his guise as an attractive man, but Taphao Thong showed no interest. Undeterred, Chalawan enchanted her with a love spell, and she agreed to become his wife.

Meanwhile, the ruler of the city was grief-stricken by the loss of his daughter. So, he announced that he was looking for a warrior who could put an end to the crocodile. Moreover, if this warrior could return his daughter to him, he would be awarded half of the ruler's wealth and permitted to marry his other daughter, Taphao Kaew. Volunteers appeared from across the land, but none could slay Chalawan, and all met their end in his belly.

Eventually, a young man named Krai Thong, who was well trained in incantations against crocodiles, volunteered to vanquish Chalawan and rescue Taphao Thong. Krai Thong paddled his boat down the river from Nonthaburi Province to Phichit armed with a magic knife and spear he had received from his mentor. As Krai Thong made his way toward the cave, Chalawan dreamed of fire and of water flooding into the caverns, after which an angel appeared and swiftly slit his throat with a horrifying splatter, jolting him to his senses. He told his grandfather of this dream, who sensed immediately the danger his grandson was in. So, he advised Chalawan to remain in the cave for seven days in meditation. Chalawan ordered a servant to blockade the mouth of the cave with a boulder and began meditating as his grandfather had counselled.

วันหนึ่งชาละวันออกจากถ้ำไปเจอสองสาวพี่น้องชื่อตะเภาแก้วกับ
ตะเภาทอง กำลังว่ายน้ำเล่นอยู่ในแม่น้ำ ทั้ง 2 คนเป็นลูกสาวของเจ้า
เมืองพิจิตร ชาละวันเห็นความงามของตะเภาทองก็เกิดหลงใหลจึงคาบ
ตะเภาทองแล้วดำดิ่งลงไปยังถ้ำ เมื่อเข้าถ้ำแล้วชาละวันก็กลายเป็นหนุ่ม
รูปงาม ตะเภาทองฟื้นขึ้นในถ้ำก็ตกตะลึงในความสวยงามของถ้ำ และชา
ละวันก็เดินเข้ามาในรูปของชายหนุ่มรูปงาม แต่ตะเภาทองไม่สนใจ ชาละ
วันเลยใช้ร่ายมนต์เสน่ห์ทำให้นางหลงรักและยอมเป็นภรรยา

ฝ่ายเจ้าเมืองหลังจากลูกสาวถูกจระเข้จับตัวไปก็โศกเศร้าเป็นอย่างมาก
จึงได้ประกาศหาคนที่สามารถปราบจระเข้ได้ ถ้านำลูกสาวกลับมาได้จะได้
ทรัพย์สมบัติครึ่งหนึ่งและได้แต่งงานกับตะเภาแก้วลูกสาวอีกคนหนึ่ง
ทำให้มีคนอาสามาปราบจระเข้หลายคนจากทั่วสารทิศ แต่ก็ไม่มีใครปราบ
ชาละวันได้และกลายเป็นอาหารของชาละวันทุกคน

ขณะนั้นมีชายหนุ่มรูปงามชื่อไกรทองเรียนคาถาอาคมปราบจระเข้จน
แก่กล้า เขาอาสาจะไปปราบพญาจระเข้ชาละวันและนำตะเภาทองกลับขึ้น
มา ไกรทองล่องเรือมาตามแม่น้ำจากจังหวัดนนทบุรีจนมาถึงเมืองพิจิตร
พร้อมกับมีดอาคมและหอกวิเศษที่ได้มาจากอาจารย์ของเขา ก่อนที่ไกร
ทองจะเดินทางมาถึง ชาละวันฝันว่ามีไฟไหม้และน้ำท่วมทะลักเข้าถ้ำ
ทันใดนั้นมีเทวดาองค์หนึ่งฟันคอของเขาขาดกระเด็น ชาละวันจึงสะดุ้ง
ตื่นขึ้นมา เขานำเรื่องความฝันไปเล่าให้ปู่ฟัง ปู่รู้ทันทีว่าหลานกำลังตก
อยู่ในอันตราย จึงสั่งให้ชาละวันจำศีลอยู่ในถ้ำ 7 วัน ชาละวันเกิดความ
กลัวจึงสั่งให้บริวารนำหินมาปิดปากถ้ำไว้อย่างแน่นหนา และเริ่มถือศีล
ตามคำแนะนำของปู่

Meanwhile, Krai Thong had begun making offerings to the spirits and masters as a prelude to his ceremonious battle with the crocodile. Krai Thong paddled his raft north to the entrance of Chalawan's cave, casting spells all the way. Due to the power of these incantations, Chalawan, who was in his cave meditating, become restless and uneasy to the point where he could barely sit still. In the end, because of his savage nature and inexperience with meditation, Chalawan was unable to resist the spells' provocation and burst out of his cave. He transformed into a crocodile and erupted out of the water to do battle with Krai Thong. Chalawan lunged onto Krai Thong's raft from behind, snapping it into splinters as he did so. But Krai Thong leapt immediately onto Chalawan's back, plunging his spear between the beast's shoulders. The spear's supernatural power caused Chalawan's diamond-like teeth to weaken, and the wounded creature fled quickly back to his cave.

Upon Chalawan's retreat, Krai Thong climbed onto the bank of the river and began casting spells using a magic candle. The water immediately parted, clearing a path to the cave. Upon entering the cavern, Krai Thong encountered the wounded Chalawan. Once again, the battle commenced, but it ended quickly. Krai Thong's magic knife pierced the already weakened crocodile's heart, killing him. With Chalawan dead, Taphao Thong was released from his spell, and Krai Thong brought her back to dry land. The ruler of the city was overjoyed to see that his daughter was still alive, so he arranged a wedding for Krai Thong and Taphao Kaew and bequeathed upon Krai Thong half of his wealth. Moreover, he allowed him to take Taphao Thong as a second wife.

ฝ่ายไกรทองได้เริ่มบวงสรวงเทวดาฟ้าดินและครูบาอาจารย์เพื่อเริ่มพิธี
ปราบจระเข้ ไกรทองล่องแพไปอยู่เหนือปากถ้ำชาละวันและร่ายคาถา
ด้วยฤทธิ์ของคาถานี้ทำให้ชาละวันที่นั่งสมาธิบำเพ็ญศีลอยู่เกิดความร้อน
รุ่มกระสับกระส่าย แทบจะนั่งอยู่ไม่ได้ แต่สุดท้ายด้วยความที่มีนิสัยดุร้าย
และไม่เคยนั่งสมาธิบำเพ็ญศีลมาก่อน ชาละวันก็ทนแรงยั่วยุจากคาถาไม่
ไหวจึงพุ่งออกจากถ้ำแปลงกายเป็นจระเข้ขึ้นมาบนผิวถ้ำสู้กับไกรทอง ชา
ละวันพุ่งขึ้นมาบนแพจากด้านหลังของไกรทอง กระชากแพแตกกระจาย
แต่ไกรทองก็กระโดดขึ้นหลังชาละวันทันทีแทงหอกเข้าไปกลางหลังชาละ
วัน ฤทธิ์อาคมของหอกทำให้เขี้ยวเพชรของชาละวันเสื่อม ชาละวันได้รับ
บาดเจ็บสาหัสและรีบหนีกลับไปที่ถ้ำของตัวเองทันที

เมื่อชาละวันล่าถอยเข้าถ้ำ ไกรทองจึงขึ้นฝั่งและเริ่มร่ายมนต์คาถาใช้
วิชาเทียนระเบิดน้ำเปิดทางน้ำ ตามเข้าไปในถ้ำทันที เมื่อไกรทองเข้ามา
ในถ้ำได้พบกับชาละวันที่บาดเจ็บอยู่ การต่อสู้จึงเริ่มขึ้นอีกครั้ง แต่การ
ต่อสู้ก็จบลงอย่างรวดเร็ว เพราะชาละวันที่บาดเจ็บสาหัสอยู่ถูกมีดอาคม
แทงสิ้นใจ เมื่อชาละวันตายมนต์เสน่ห์ที่สะกดจิตตะเภาทองอยู่ก็คลาย
ออก ไกรทองจึงพานางตะเภาทองกลับขึ้นมาบนบก เจ้าเมืองดีใจมากที่
ลูกสาวยังไม่ตาย จากนั้นจึงจัดงานแต่งงานให้ไกรทองกับตะเภาแก้ว
และมอบทรัพย์สมบัติให้ครึ่งหนึ่งและยกนางตะเภาทองให้เป็นเมียไกร
ทองอีกคน

Vocabulary

1	ถ้ำ	thâm	cave
2	ศักดิ์สิทธิ์	sàk sìt	sacred
3	กลายร่าง	glaay râang	to change/transform into
4	มนุษย์	má-nút	human
5	พญา, ราชา	phá yaa, raa-chaa	king
6	อันธพาล	an thá paan	scoundrel, nasty character
7	คาบ	khâap	to snatch up/hold in one's mouth
8	ร่ายมนต์	ràay mon	to enchant
9	โศกเศร้า	sòhk sâo	depressed, grief-stricken
10	อาสา	aa săa	to volunteer
11	ปราบ	pràap	to vanquish
12	หอกวิเศษ	hàwk wí sèht	magic spear
13	เทวดา	theh-wá-daa	spirit
14	บริวาร	baw-rí-waan	servant
15	คาถา	khaa-thăa	magic spell
16	บำเพ็ญศีล	bam phen sĭin	to meditate
17	กระสับกระส่าย	grà-sàp-grà-sàay	to fidget, be unable to sit still
18	เสื่อม	sùeam	to weaken (supernatural power)
19	บาดเจ็บ	bàat jèp	wound (injury)
20	การต่อสู้	gaan tàw sûu	battle
21	สิ้นใจ	sîn jai	dead
22	มนต์เสน่ห์	mon sà-nèh	spell
23	คลาย	khlaay	to release
24	บก	bòk	(dry) land
25	ทรัพย์สมบัติ	sáp sŏm bàt	wealth

Culture Notes

Khaa-thǎa aa-khom (incantations) are rituals derived from the 18 liberal arts teachings of ancient India, which have been part of the Thai belief system for many years. They have a profound influence on the lives of Thai people from birth to death. They refer mostly to beliefs based on supernatural power and inspiration and relate to sacred items, miracles, and supernatural mysteries. In some cases, incantations might be learned as spells for protection, or they may even be used for darker purposes.

Comprehension Questions

1. ชาละวันมีนิสัยอย่างไร
2. ก่อนที่ไกรทองจะเดินทางมาถึงชาละวันฝันอะไร
3. ไกรทองใช้อะไรต่อสู้กับชาละวัน

Writing Activity

เขียนเปรียบเทียบความเหมือนและแตกต่างของ "ไกรทอง" และ "ชาละวัน" ว่าทั้งสองคนเหมือนกันอย่างไรและแตกต่างกันอย่างไร

Compare and contrast Krai Thaong and Chalawan. How are they similar? How are they different?

The Golden Goby Fish

There was once a wealthy fisherman who had two wives: Khanittha, with whom he had a daughter named Ueay, and Khanitthi, with whom he had two daughters named Ai and Ee. Every morning, the man would go out on the river in search of fish, and his wives would take turns as oarswomen. After they had caught enough fish each day, they would make their way to the market and sell off their haul before returning home.

One day, Khanittha was on rowing duty while her husband fished. He cast his net repeatedly throughout the day, but time and again, he caught only a single goby fish. Each time, he would release the fish, only to see it again when next he drew up his net. Eventually, he gave up and decided to return home with his lone catch. Khanittha took pity on the fish and pleaded with her husband to set it free. This infuriated him, and in his rage he lashed out, sending Khanittha tumbling into the water. Khanittha, who could not swim, promptly drowned.

ปลาบู่ทอง

เศรษฐีคนหนึ่งมีอาชีพหาปลา มีภรรยา 2 คน คนแรกชื่อ "ขนิษฐา" ซึ่ง
มีลูกสาวชื่อ "เอื้อย" ส่วนภรรยาคนที่สองชื่อ "ขนิษฐี" มีลูกสาวสองคน
ชื่อ "อ้าย" กับ "อี่" ทุกเช้าเศรษฐีจะออกไปหาปลาในแม่น้ำและจะมี
ภรรยาสองคนผลัดกันเป็นคนพายเรือ หลังจากได้ปลามากพอในแต่ละวัน
ก็จะนำไปขายที่ตลาดก่อนกลับบ้าน

อยู่มาวันหนึ่งนางขนิษฐาทำหน้าที่เป็นคนพายเรือให้สามีในขณะหา
ปลา ตลอดทั้งวันเหวี่ยงแหไปกี่ครั้งก็จับปลาได้แต่ปลาบู่ตัวเดียวเท่านั้น
พอเขาปล่อยลงไปในน้ำ แต่ไม่นานปลาบู่ตัวเดิมก็ติดแหขึ้นมาอีก สุดท้าย
เศรษฐีก็ตัดสินใจจะเอาปลาบู่ที่จับได้เพียงตัวเดียวกลับบ้าน นางขนิษฐา
เกิดความสงสารปลาบู่ ขอให้เศรษฐีปล่อยปลาไป แต่เขาไม่พอใจเกิด
บันดาลโทสะตบตีนางขนิษฐาและผลักตกน้ำไป นางขนิษฐาจึงจมน้ำตาย
เพราะว่ายน้ำไม่เป็น

When he returned home, he told Ueay that her mother had run off with another man and that she would not be coming back. Ueay was heartbroken to have lost her mother. To make matters worse, Khanitthi now saw fit to mistreat her step-daughter without reservation. She forced Ueay to do all of the household chores, while her own daughters were allowed to merely sit back and watch.

The drowned Khanittha was soon reborn as a golden goby fish, which each day, would swim to the water's edge in the hope that Ueay would appear. One day, Ueay was missing her mother so terribly that she crumpled down by the river and began to sob. It was then that she saw the golden goby fish, who recounted to her daughter all that had taken place. Ueay felt sorry for her mother and, from then on, would regularly come to speak with her and feed her, hoping that it might help ease her pain.

It was not long, however, before Khanitthi and her two daughters found out about the golden goby fish and hatched a plan. While Ueay was out tending the cattle in the field, the three of them caught the fish and killed it, feeding it to their dogs and cats. When Ueay returned to the river, her mother was nowhere to be found. All that was left of her were a few scattered golden scales. Ueay was heartbroken. She buried the scales in the ground and prayed that her mother would be born again as a nightshade.

By a spirit's blessing, a beautiful nightshade suddenly sprouted there before her. Each day after that, a contented Ueay would make her way to the tree to speak with her mother and pay her respect. Unfortunately, Khanitthi and her daughters had spied Ueay on one of her visits to the nightshade. So, they picked and ate all of its fruit, ripped it out of the soil by its roots, and tossed it away. Undeterred, Ueay gathered up all of the scattered seeds she could find, buried them in the forest, and prayed for her mother to be born again as a silver and gold bodhi tree that she might continue to pay her respects. And by the spirits' grace, a silver and gold bodhi tree instantly sprang up from the earth.

One day, King Phrommathat was passing by and noticed the bodhi tree. He decided that he would very much like it in his palace, but try as they might, no one in his caravan was able to uproot the tree. So, the king offered a reward to whoever could remove it from the earth. When Khanitthi and her two daughters got wind of this, they hurried to the tree and tried

เมื่อกลับถึงบ้านเศรษฐีก็หลอกเอื้อยว่า แม่หนีตามผู้ชายไป ไม่กลับมา อีกแล้ว เอื้อยเสียใจมากที่แม่หายไป และนับแต่นั้นมาเอื้อยก็ถูกนาง ขนิษฐ์กลั่นแกล้งใช้ให้ทำงานในบ้านทุกอย่าง ตรงข้ามกับลูกสาวทั้งสอง คนที่ไม่ต้องทำอะไรเลย

หลังจากจมน้ำตาย นางขนิษฐาก็ไปเกิดเป็นปลาบู่ทองและว่ายน้ำมา รอเอื้อยที่ท่าน้ำหน้าบ้านทุกวัน วันหนึ่งเอื้อยคิดถึงแม่มากจึงไปนั่งร้องไห้ ท่าน้ำ ก็ได้พบปลาบู่ทองซึ่งเป็นแม่ของตัวเอง แม่ปลาบู่ทองเล่าเรื่อง ทั้งหมดให้เอื้อยฟัง เมื่อรู้ความจริงเอื้อยสงสารแม่มาก จึงนำอาหารมาให้ แม่ปลาบู่ทองกินเป็นประจำและพูดคุยกับแม่เพื่อให้ลืมความทุกข์ใจ

แต่ไม่นานขนิษฐ์และลูกสาวสองคนเริ่มสงสัยและสืบดูจนรู้เรื่องของ แม่ปลาบู่ทอง ขณะที่เอื้อยออกไปเลี้ยงวัวในทุ่งนา ทั้งสามคนจึงวางแผน จับแม่ปลาบู่ทองแล้วฆ่าเพื่อเอาไปทำอาหารให้หมาและแมวกิน เอื้อยกลับ มาไม่เจอแม่ พบแต่เกล็ดปลาบู่ทอง เอื้อยเสียใจมาก จึงนำเกล็ดปลาบู่ ทองไปฝังดินแล้วอธิษฐานขอให้แม่มาเกิดเป็นต้นมะเขือ

ด้วยพรของเทวดา ทันใดนั้นต้นมะเขือก็งอกงามขึ้นมา นับแต่นั้นมา เอื้อยก็มีความสุขที่ได้มากราบไหว้และพูดคุยกับแม่ที่ต้นมะเขือทุกวัน แต่ โชคร้ายนางขนิษฐ์และลูกสาวทั้งสองแอบมาเห็นอีก จึงเก็บผลมะเขือมา กินแล้วถอนต้นมะเขือทิ้ง เอื้อยยังไม่ละความพยายาม นำเม็ดมะเขือที่ เก็บได้ไปฝังดินไว้ในป่าแล้วอธิษฐานขอให้แม่เกิดเป็นต้นโพธิ์เงินโพธิ์ทอง เพื่อจะได้กราบไหว้บูชา และด้วยพรของเทวดาต้นโพธิ์เงินโพธิ์ทองก็ งอกงามขึ้นทันที

วันหนึ่งพระเจ้าพรหมทัตผ่านมาเห็นต้นโพธิ์เงินโพธิ์ทอง อยากนำไป ปลูกในวัง แต่ไม่มีใครสามารถเคลื่อนต้นโพธิ์เงินโพธิ์ทองนี้ได้เลย เขาจึง ประกาศจะให้รางวัลหากมีใครสามารถทำได้ เมื่อนางขนิษฐ์และลูกสาว สองคนรู้ข่าวก็มาร่วมถอนต้นโพธิ์เงินโพธิ์ทอง แต่ทำไม่ได้ แต่พอเอื้อยมา

with all of their collective might to dislodge its roots, but their efforts were in vain. When it was Ueay's turn to try, she began by praying to her mother for permission, which allowed her to successfully lift the tree from the soil. The king became enamored with Ueay, who had proven her virtue. He thus made her his queen and took her to live with him in his palace.

When Khanitthi and her two daughters learned of Ueay's appointment, they were wild with envy. Hoping to trick her, they sent word that her father was deathly ill and would not live long. Ueay fell for their ruse and immediately rushed back to visit her father. Khanitthi, meanwhile, had prepared a vat of boiling water and placed it in front of the house's entrance. In her haste to enter the house, Ueay did not notice the boiling water and was instantly killed. Khanitthi then had Ai impersonate Ueay and return to the palace in her place.

Ueay, meanwhile, was reborn as a parakeet and eventually flew back to the palace. The king sensed the bird's intelligence and kept her in a gilded cage, where he would talk with her night and day. This displeased Ai, who snatched the parakeet out of her cage and brought her to the palace cook to pluck and boil. But after stripping the bird of its plumage, the cook left her alone on the table, which gave the featherless parakeet the opportunity to escape and hide herself in a nearby mouse hole. The cook, fearing punishment for having lost the bird, snuck out and bought another to prepare for Ai. Ueay remained in the mouse hole until her feathers had grown back fully and then flew into the forest. There, she encountered a hermit, who took pity on her and restored her human form. He then drew a picture of a boy, upon which he cast a spell, bringing it to life for Ueay to raise as her son.

After many years had passed and her boy had grown, she requested entry into the palace to meet with the king and explain all that had happened. The king was happy to see that Ueay was still alive and sentenced Khanitthi and both of her daughters to death. Ueay and the bodhi tree lived lives of tranquility from that day onward.

อธิษฐานขออนุญาตแม่ ทำให้เอื้อยสามารถถอนต้นโพธิ์เงินโพธิ์ทองได้
สำเร็จ พระเจ้าพรหมทัตรู้สึกถูกชะตาเอื้อยและคิดว่าเอื้อยมีบุญบารมี ก็
เลยแต่งตั้งให้เป็นมเหสีและพาไปอยู่ในวัง

ในขณะเดียวกันนางขนิษฐ์และลูกสาวทั้งสองก็เกิดความอิจฉาริษยา
อย่างมากที่ได้รู้ข่าวว่าเอื้อยได้กลายเป็นมเหสีไปแล้ว จึงออกอุบายส่งข่าว
ไปบอกเอื้อยว่าพ่อป่วยหนักใกล้จะตายแล้ว เอื้อยหลงเชื่อทันทีที่รู้ข่าวก็
รีบกลับมาเยี่ยมพ่อที่บ้าน นางขนิษฐ์ได้เตรียมกับดักไว้ ด้วยความรีบร้อน
ทำให้เอื้อยตกลงไปในกระทะน้ำเดือดใต้ถุนบ้านตายทันที จากนั้นก็ให้
ลูกสาวชื่อ "อ้าย" ปลอมตัวเป็นเอื้อยและกลับวัง

หลังจากถูกฆ่าตาย เอื้อยก็ไปเกิดเป็นนกแขกเต้าแล้วบินกลับเข้าวัง
พระเจ้าพรหมทัตเห็นนกแขกเต้าแสนรู้ก็เลยเลี้ยงไว้ในกรงทองและพูดคุย
ด้วยเสมอ อ้ายเห็นแล้วก็ไม่พอใจ จับนกแขกเต้าไปให้แม่ครัวถอนขนและ
ต้มกิน แต่แม่ครัวถอนขนนกแขกเต้าแล้ววางทิ้งไว้บนโต๊ะ นกแขกเต้าที่
ไม่มีขนจึงสบโอกาสหนีเข้าไปซ่อนตัวอยู่ในโพรงหนู เมื่อหานกแขกเต้าไม่
พบและกลัวจะมีความผิด แม่ครัวจึงไปหาซื้อนกอื่นมาทำอาหารให้อ้าย
นกแขกเต้าอาศัยอยู่ในโพรงหนูจนกระทั่งขนขึ้นเต็มตัวก็บินเข้าป่าจนมา
พบกับพระฤๅษี ด้วยความสงสารพระฤๅษีจึงช่วยชุบชีวิตนกแขกเต้าให้
กลับเป็นคนตามเดิม แล้วยังวาดรูปเด็กชายและใช้คาถาเสกให้เป็นคนเพื่อ
ให้เป็นลูกชายของเอื้อย

ผ่านไปหลายปี เมื่อลูกชายโตขึ้นจึงขอเข้าไปในวังเพื่อพบกับพระเจ้า
พรหมทัตและเล่าความจริงทั้งหมดให้ฟัง พระเจ้าพรหมทัตดีใจที่เอื้อยยัง
มีชีวิตอยู่และให้ไปรับเอื้อยกลับวัง จากนั้นก็สั่งประหารชีวิตนางขนิษฐ์
และลูกสาวทั้งสอง ส่วนเอื้อยและต้นโพธิ์เงินโพธิ์ทองก็มีชีวิตที่สงบสุข
นับแต่นั้นมา

Vocabulary

1	เศรษฐี	**sèt thĕe**	wealthy man
2	ปลาบู่	**plaa bùu**	goby fish
3	สงสาร	**sŏng săan**	to pity
4	กลั่นแกล้ง	**glàn glâehng**	to mistreat
5	สืบ	**sùehp**	to find out
6	วางแผน	**waang phăehn**	to make/hatch a plan
7	เกล็ดปลา	**glèt plaa**	scales
8	ฝัง	**făng**	to bury
9	อธิษฐาน	**à thít thăan**	to pray
10	ต้นมะเขือ	**tôn má khŭea**	nightshade (eggplant)
11	ไม่ละความพยายาม	**khwaam phá-yaa-yaam**	to be undeterred
12	ต้นโพธิ์เงินโพธิ์ทอง	**tôn phoh ngerrn phoh thawng**	silver and gold bodhi tree
13	กราบไหว้บูชา	**gràap wâi buu chaa**	to pay one's respects
14	งอกงาม	**ngâwk ngaam**	to grow, sprout
15	ถูกชะตา	**thùuk chá taa**	to be enamored with
16	บุญบารมี	**bun baa rá mii**	virtue
17	อิจฉาริษยา	**ìt chăa rít sà yăa**	envy
18	หลงเชื่อ	**lŏng chûea**	to fall for (a trick/ruse)
19	กับดัก	**gàp dàk**	trap
20	ความรีบร้อน	**rîip ráwn**	to revise
21	ปลอมตัว	**plawm tua**	to impersonate
22	ชุบชีวิต	**chúp chii wít**	to revive, restore
23	คาถา	**khaa thăa**	magic spell
24	ประหารชีวิต	**prà-hăan chii-wít**	to sentence to death
25	สงบสุข	**sà ngòp sùk**	tranquility

Culture Notes

The **Bodhi** tree is native to India and plays an important role in Buddhism because it was under such a tree that the Buddha attained enlightenment. The Bodhi tree therefore is known as the "tree of enlightenment" (*Bodhi* translates as "site of knowing" or "site of enlightenment") and is also highly revered by Buddhists, Brahmans, and Hindus. For Thai people, the Bodhi tree symbolizes peace and tranquility. One can often see Bodhi trees planted in the vicinity of ancient Buddhist temples. In the past, it was taboo to cut down Bodhi trees and it was thought that those who broke this rule would suffer misfortune.

Comprehension Questions

1. เมื่อนำเกล็ดปลาบู่ทองไปฝังดินแล้ว เอื้อยอธิษฐานขอให้แม่มาเกิดเป็นอะไร
2. ทำไมพระเจ้าพรหมทัตแต่งตั้งให้เอื้อยเป็นมเหสีและพาไปอยู่ในวัง
3. หลังจากเอื้อยถูกฆ่าตาย เอื้อยเกิดเป็นอะไร

Writing Activity

เขียนอีเมล์ถึงคนที่คุณรู้จัก (เช่น เพื่อน เพื่อนที่โรงเรียน หรือคนใน ครอบครัว) เล่าให้ฟังถึงสิ่งที่ได้เรียนรู้จาก "เอื้อย"

Write an email to someone you know (e.g., a friend, fellow classmate, or family member) telling them about what you have learned about Ueay.

The Adventures of the Boy in the Golden Conch

There was once a king named Yossawimon, whose wife, Janthewi, gave birth to a conch. The king's first concubine, Jantha, saw this as an opportunity to oust the queen and usurp her position. She bribed the royal soothsayer to prophesize that the conch would bring ruin on the city. King Yossawimon fell for the ruse and exiled Janthewi and the conch. Together, the woman and the conch wandered until they came to the forest outside of the city, where they encountered an elderly couple and their farm. The farmers took pity on the drifters and allowed them to stay in their home. Every day, when Janthewi set out to work in the field, a tiny boy would sneak out of the conch and help with the household chores. Once he had finished, he would slip stealthily back into the shell.

สังข์ทอง

"ท้าวยศวิมล" มีมเหสีชื่อ "นางจันท์เทวี" และมีสนมเอกชื่อ "นางจันทา"
ต่อมานางจันท์เทวีตั้งครรภ์และคลอดลูกออกมาเป็น "หอยสังข์" นางจัน
ทาจึงออกอุบายติดสินบนให้โหรหลวงทำนายว่าหอยสังข์จะทำให้บ้าน
เมืองเกิดความหายนะ ท้าวยศวิมลหลงเชื่อจึงเนรเทศนางจันท์เทวีและ
หอยสังข์ออกจากเมือง นางจันท์เทวีพาหอยสังข์เดินทางเร่ร่อนไปจนถึง
ชายป่านอกเมืองและได้พบกับตายายคู่หนึ่งซึ่งเป็นชาวไร่ ตากับยาย
สงสารจึงชวนให้พักอยู่ด้วยกัน ทุกวันเมื่อนางจันท์เทวีออกจากบ้านไปทำ
ไร่ ลูกน้อยในหอยสังข์จะแอบออกมาช่วยทำงานบ้านให้เรียบร้อยทุกครั้ง
พอทำเสร็จก็กลับเข้าไปในหอยสังข์ตามเดิม

Upon returning to the house, Janthewi was always surprised to find her chores finished. She wondered who could possibly have done them. So one day, she made a show of departing for the field as usual, but then swiftly doubled back and returned to the house, where she spied the small boy as he crawled out of the shell and set about the day's housework. Elated, Janthewi joyfully embraced the child. She then smashed the conch and named him Sang Thong.

When King Yossawimon learned that the infant in the conch had been a boy, he considered allowing Janthewi to return. But Jantha became jealous and urged the king to reconsider, warning him that the conch would bring misfortune on the city. The king was deceived once again and ordered Janthewi and Prince Sang Thong to be put on a raft and sent out to sea. While afloat, they encountered a mighty storm that split the raft asunder. Sang Thong was set adrift and washed ashore in the city of the ogres.

The ogress Phanthurat discovered Prince Sang Thong in the remains of his boat and was overcome with compassion. So, she took him in and raised him, assuming human form so that Sang Thong would not discover what she really was. It was thus that Sang Thong grew up with Phanthurat. One day, when the ogress went out in search of food, Sang Thong stole into the castle, which he was forbidden to enter. When he did, he found a magical well of gold, forest-dweller armor, golden shoes, and a staff. He also saw piles of human and animal bones, which revealed to him the truth about Phanthurat. Sang Thong thus dipped himself in the golden well, donned the forest-dweller armor and golden shoes, snatched the staff, and soared away.

เมื่อนางจันท์เทวีกลับมาก็แปลกใจว่าใครมาช่วยทำงานและอยากรู้ว่า
เป็นใคร วันหนึ่งจึงทำทีออกจากบ้านไปป่าเหมือนเช่นเคยแต่แล้วก็ย้อน
กลับมาที่บ้าน นางจันท์เทวีจึงได้เห็นลูกน้อยในหอยสังข์ออกมาทำงาน
บ้าน นางจันท์เทวีดีใจกอดลูกชายด้วยความยินดี จากนั้นก็ทุบหอยสังข์
ทิ้งและตั้งชื่อให้ลูกชายว่า "สังข์ทอง"

ต่อมาเมื่อท้าวยศวิมลรู้ข่าวว่าลูกน้อยในหอยสังข์เป็นลูกชายก็อยากจะ
รับนางจันท์เทวีกลับมา แต่นางจันทาเกิดความอิจฉาจึงยุยงว่าหอยสังข์
เป็นกาลกิณีต่อบ้านเมือง ท้าวยศวิมลหลงเชื่อจึงสั่งให้จับนางจันท์เทวี
และพระสังข์ทองใส่แพลอยไปในทะเล เมื่ออยู่ในทะเลเกิดพายุใหญ่ทำให้
แพแตก สังข์ทองถูกคลื่นซัดลอยไปถึงเมืองยักษ์

นางยักษ์พันธุรัตเห็นพระสังข์ทองในเรือเกิดความรักใคร่เอ็นดู จึงนำ
พระสังข์ทองมาเลี้ยงดูโดยนางยักษ์พันธุรัตได้แปลงร่างเป็นคนเพื่อไม่ให้
พระสังข์ทองรู้ว่าตัวเองเป็นยักษ์ พระสังข์ทองก็เติบโตอยู่กับนางยักษ์
พันธุรัต วันหนึ่งนางพันธุรัตออกไปหาอาหาร พระสังข์ทองจึงแอบขึ้นไป
บนปราสาทที่ห้ามไว้ เขาได้พบกับบ่อเงินบ่อทอง เกราะรูปเงาะป่า รองเท้า
ทอง ไม้พลอง และรู้ความจริงว่านางพันธุรัตเป็นยักษ์เพราะเห็นกระดูก
สัตว์และคนเป็นจำนวนมาก พระสังข์ทองจึงลงไปชุบตัวในบ่อทอง สวม
เกราะรูปเงาะป่ากับรองเท้าทอง และขโมยไม้พลองแล้วเหาะหนีไป

Sang Thong journeyed on until he reached Samon City, which was ruled by King Samon and Queen Montha with their seven daughters. One day, King Samon held an event at which all seven of his daughters were to choose a marriage partner. All did so except for the youngest, Rotjana, who chose no one. King Samon thus summoned all of the men in the city so that Rotjana could take her pick from among them. Sang Thong also attended, still clad in his forest-dweller armor. When the time came for Rotjana to make her choice, she sensed Sang Thong's golden form beneath his armor and flung her garland toward him, thus making him her partner. King Samon was furious at this and sent Rotjana to live in the woods with her forest-dweller husband.

The deity Indra saw the events in Samon City from heaven and decided to help. He challenged King Samon to a polo match. If the king were to lose, he would be obliged to cede his city to the god. Samon sent his six sons-in-law to compete, but each was summarily defeated. He was ultimately forced to swallow his pride and reluctantly summoned the forest dweller to help. Sang Thong relented. He removed his forest-dweller armor, donned his golden sandals, and flew to the match to defeat Indra.

After finishing his task in Samon City, Indra went on to expose the wicked deception of King Yossawimon's concubine, Jantha. He then ordered the king to fetch Janthewi and Sang Thong and allow them to return to the city. When the three of them, along with Rotjana, returned to Yossawimon, the king ordered Jantha executed, and Sang Thong ruled the city thereafter.

พระสังข์ทองเดินทางมาถึงเมืองสามลซึ่งมี "ท้าวสามล"และ "นาง มณฑา" เป็นเจ้าเมืองและมีลูกสาวถึง 7 คน วันหนึ่งท้าวสามลจัดงาน เลือกคู่ให้ลูกสาวทั้งเจ็ดคน ในวันนั้นลูกสาว 6 คน ต่างเลือกคู่ครองได้ ยกเว้นนางรจนาลูกสาวคนสุดท้ายที่ไม่ได้เลือกใครเป็นคู่ครอง ท้าว สามลจึงประกาศให้ชายทุกคนในเมืองเข้ามาให้ลูกสาวเลือก พระสังข์ ทองในรูปเงาะป่าก็เข้ามาด้วย เมื่อถึงเวลาเลือกคู่ บุญบันดาลให้นาง รจนาเห็นรูปทองของพระสังข์ภายใต้เกราะของเงาะป่า นางจึงเสี่ยงพวง มาลัยเลือกเงาะป่า ท้าวสามลโกรธมากจึงขับไล่นางรจนาให้ไปอยู่ที่ กระท่อมในป่ากับเจ้าเงาะ

พระอินทร์ซึ่งอยู่บนสวรรค์รู้เห็นเหตุการณ์ในเมืองสามลจึงออกอุบาย ช่วยเหลือโดยท้าให้ท้าวสามลออกมาแข่งตีคลี หากท้าวสามลแพ้จะต้องยก เมืองสามลให้ ท้าวสามลส่งหกเขยไปแข่งตีคลีกับพระอินทร์แต่ก็แพ้ ราบคาบ จึงจำใจเรียกเจ้าเงาะให้มาช่วยตีคลี เจ้าเงาะใจอ่อนยอมถอดรูป เงาะเป็นพระสังข์ทองใส่รองเท้าทองเหาะขึ้นไปตีคลีกับพระอินทร์จนชนะ

หลังจากเสร็จภารกิจที่เมืองสามลแล้ว พระอินทร์ได้เปิดโปงความชั่ว ของนางจันทาผู้เป็นสนมเอก พร้อมกับสั่งให้ท้าวยศวิมลไปรับนางจันท์ เทวีและพระสังข์ทองกลับมา หลังจากนั้น ท้าวยศวิมล นางจันท์เทวี พระ สังข์ทองกับนางรจนาได้เดินทางกลับเมืองยศวิมล ท้าวยศวิมลได้สั่ง ประหารนางจันทา และให้พระสังข์ทองปกครองบ้านเมืองต่อไป

Vocabulary

1	สนมเอก	sà nŏm èhk	first concubine
2	หอยสังข์	hŏy săng	conch
3	สินบน	sĭn bon	bribe
4	หายนะ	hăay yá ná	ruin (disaster)
5	เนรเทศ	neh rá thêht	to exile
6	ทุบ	thúp	to hit, smash
7	ยุยง	yú yong	to urge
8	กาลกิณี	gaa lá gì nii	misfortune
9	หลงเชื่อ	lŏng chûea	to be deceived
10	ปราสาท	praa sàat	castle
11	เกราะ	gràw	armor
12	ไม้พลอง	mái phlawng	staff
13	ชุบตัว	chúp tua	to dip oneself (in something)
14	เหาะ	hàw	to soar
15	เลือกคู่	lûeak khûu	to choose a marriage partner.
16	พวงมาลัย	phuang maa lai	garland
17	พระอินทร์	phrá-in	Indra (Hindu/Buddhist deity)
18	สวรรค์	sà wăn	heaven
19	แข่ง	khàehng	to compete
20	ตีคลี	tii khlii	to play *khli* (a game similar to polo)
21	เขย	khĕhy	son-in-law
22	แพ้	phâeh	to be defeated
23	จำใจ	jam jai	to be reluctant
24	ใจอ่อน	jai àwn	to relent, give in
25	ภารกิจ	phaa-rá-gìt	task
26	ความชั่ว	khwaam chûa	wickedness

Culture Notes

The god Indra is the highest deity in Buddhism who rules over Trayastrimsha heaven. Indra is a moral deity and creates only virtue and goodness as a disciple of the Buddha. Thai people believe that Indra is to be worshipped as the king of the highest heaven and have included "Indra" in the names of various culturally important sites. Originally, Indra was depicted as having a sturdy body, golden hair, beard, and nails, eyes all over his body, and four hands. Later, Indra is depicted as having a more beautiful face and body, which went from being red to ivory and finally to green, which is how he is depicted today.

Comprehension Questions

1. เมื่อนางจันท์เทวีออกจากบ้านไปทำไร่ ลูกน้อยในหอยสังข์จะแอบออกมาทำอะไร

2. พระสังข์ทองรู้ความจริงว่านางพันธุรัตเป็นยักษ์เพราะอะไร

3. หากท้าวสามลแพ้แข่งตีคลีกับพระอินทร์ เขาจะต้องทำอะไร

Writing Activity

สมมติว่าถ้าตัวละครคนหนึ่งทำสิ่งที่แตกต่างไปจากในนิทาน ตอนจบของเรื่องจะเปลี่ยนไปอย่างไร

Imagine a certain character in this story did something totally different, what would the ending of this story be?

Prince Chaiya Chet

Jampa Thong was the daughter of King Aphainurat, the ruler of the city of Wesali. Her name, which meant "golden champak flower," had been given to her because when she cried, she shed champak flowers in place of tears. Jampa Thong had been raising a crocodile in the palace, which once grown, became fierce and terrorized the villagers. This enraged King Aphainurat, who responded by promptly exiling Jampa Thong from the city. Accompanied by her pet cat, Jampa Thong wandered the forest until she encountered an ogre named Nonthayak. Startled, she fled, running until she happened upon a hermit, whom she begged to provide shelter for her and her feline companion.

ไชยเชษฐ์

"ท้าวอภัยนุราช" เจ้าเมืองเวสาลีมีลูกสาวชื่อ "จำปาทอง" เพราะเมื่อ
ร้องไห้จะมีดอกจำปาทองร่วงลงมา จำปาทองเลี้ยงจระเข้ไว้ในวัง เมื่อ
จระเข้โตขึ้น ก็ดุร้ายเที่ยวไล่กัดชาวเมืองจนเดือดร้อนไปทั่ว ท้าวอภัยนุราช
โกรธเคืองจึงขับไล่จำปาทองออกจากเมือง จำปาทองได้นำแมวที่เลี้ยงไว้
ติดตามไปด้วย จำปาทองกับแมวเดินพเนจรอยู่ในป่าและได้พบยักษ์ตน
หนึ่งชื่อ "นนทยักษ์" จึงตกใจกลัววิ่งหนี จนได้พบกับพระฤาษีที่ช่วยไว้
จำปาทองกับแมวจึงขออาศัยอยู่กับพระฤาษีในป่านั้น

Meanwhile, in the ogre city of Singhon, King Singhon had had a dream of another ogre presenting him with a champak flower from the forest. The flower had been the color of purest gold and marvelous to behold. He consulted his soothsayer about the dream, who proclaimed that it presaged the king having a daughter. Nonthayak heard this and told the king of the girl she had encountered living with the hermit in the woods. Singhon thus went to visit the hermit and request that Jampa Thong return with him as his daughter. She agreed, and he named her Suwincha.

Chaiya Chet was the prince of the nearby city of Heman. One day, he was out for a stroll in the woods and lost his way, accidentally wandering into Singhon. Suwincha was out admiring her garden when she happened to see the prince and so took him to meet with King Singhon. Chaiya Chet promised the city officials that if enemies attacked Heman, he would volunteer to take up arms and defeat them. In return, the king allowed the prince to take Suwincha as his wife. She thus returned with him to the city of Heman.

Back in Heman, the prince's seven concubines had become jealous of Suwincha, as they could see that she was first in the prince's heart. Suwincha soon became pregnant. But when the day of the infant's birth grew near, the seven concubines convinced Chaiya Chet that a white elephant had been seen in the forest, so he left the palace to capture it. Meanwhile, Suwincha gave birth to a son, who came into the world armed with an bow and a dagger. The seven concubines promptly seized the boy, forced him into a trunk, and buried him beneath a banyan tree in the forest. However, the spirit of the banyan tree kept the interred infant alive. When Chaiya Chet returned from his elephant hunt, his concubines told him that Suwincha had given birth to a log. The prince summarily exiled Suwincha from the kingdom for bearing him such a child. Her cat had seen what the concubines had done and so led Suwincha to the spot where her son had been buried. They unearthed the trunk from beneath the tree and took the child back to Singhon, where the king named him Narai Thibet.

"ท้าวสิงหล" เป็นยักษ์ครองเมืองสิงหล คืนหนึ่งท้าวสิงหลฝันว่า มี
ยักษ์ตนหนึ่งนำดอกจำปาจากป่ามาให้ ดอกจำปามีสีเหลืองเหมือนทองคำ
สวยงามมาก ท้าวสิงหลจึงให้โหรทำนายฝัน โหรบอกว่าท้าวสิงหลจะได้
ลูกสาว นนทยักษ์บอกท้าวสิงหลว่าพบหญิงสาวคนหนึ่งอาศัยอยู่กับพระ
ฤษีในป่า ท้าวสิงหลจึงไปหาพระฤษี และขอจำปาทองมาเป็นลูกและตั้ง
ชื่อว่า "สุวิญชา"

ฝ่าย "พระไชยเชษฐ์" เป็นลูกชายเจ้าเมืองเหมันต์ วันหนึ่งพระไชย
เชษฐ์ไปเที่ยวป่าและหลงทางเข้าไปในสวนเมืองสิงหล สุวิญชามาเที่ยวชม
สวนพบพระไชยเชษฐ์ จึงพาพระไชยเชษฐ์ไปพบท้าวสิงหลและพระไชย
เชษฐ์ขอรับราชการในเมืองสิงหล ต่อมามีข้าศึกยกทัพมาโจมตีเมืองสิงหล
พระไชยเชษฐ์อาสาสู้ศึกจนชนะ ท้าวสิงหลจึงยกสุวิญชาให้เป็นชายาของ
พระไชยเชษฐ์ พระไชยเชษฐ์จึงพาสุวิญชากลับเมืองเหมันต์

ที่เมืองเหมันต์ พระไชยเชษฐ์มีสนม 7 คน อิจฉาสุวิญชาเพราะพระ
ไชยเชษฐ์รักสุวิญชามากกว่า ต่อมาสุวิญชาตั้งครรภ์ และเมื่อใกล้ถึง
กำหนดคลอด นางสนมทั้ง 7 คน ก็ออกอุบายว่ามีช้างเผือกอยู่ในป่า พระ
ไชยเชษฐ์จึงออกไปคล้องช้างเผือก ส่วนสุวิญชาได้คลอดลูกเป็นผู้ชายมีศร
กับพระขรรค์ติดตัวมาด้วย นางสนมทั้ง 7 คน จับลูกชายของสุวิญชาใส่
หีบแล้วฝังไว้ใต้ต้นไทรในป่า เทวดาประจำต้นไม้ช่วยชีวิตเด็กชายไว้ เมื่อ
พระไชยเชษฐ์กลับจากคล้องช้างเผือก นางสนมทั้ง 7 คน โกหกว่าสุวิญ
ชาคลอดลูกเป็นท่อนไม้ พระไชยเชษฐ์จึงขับไล่สุวิญชาออกจากเมือง ขณะ
ที่นางสุวิญชาคลอดลูกนั้น แมวแอบเห็นการกระทำของนางสนมทั้ง 7
คน จึงพาสุวิญชาไปขุดหีบใต้ต้นไทรแล้วพาลูกชายกลับไปเมืองสิงหล
ท้าวสิงหลตั้งชื่อหลานชายว่า "พระนารายณ์ธิเบศร์"

Prince Chaiya Chet later realized that Suwincha had been maligned and traveled to the kingdom of Singhon to seek her out. He encountered Prince Narai Thibet, who was on a walk with his nursemaid in the woods. This adorable child looked so much like Chaiya Chet that he was convinced it must be his son, so he tried to embrace the child and offered him sweets. However, this stranger's attempt to lay hands on him enraged Narai Thibet. He drew his bow and went to shoot him through with an arrow, but his weapon burst into a billow of flowers, which floated gently down and scattered across the ground. This astonished Chaiya Chet, who prayed that if this boy was indeed his and Suwincha's son, the next arrow he loosed would transform into food. He then released an arrow from his bow, which instantly became a great feast spread across ground around them. He was thus assured of the boy's parentage.

Chaiya Chet asked the child who his mother was. The child replied that his mother was Suwincha and his father was King Singhon. Chaiya Chet then told the boy of all that had taken place. Now realizing that this man was his father, Narai Thibet took him to meet King Singhon. Chaiya Chet begged Suwincha's forgiveness, and Narai Thibet spoke to quell her anger toward his father. Suwincha eventually forgave Chaiya Chet and the three of them were able to live together happily as a family.

ต่อมาพระไชยเชษฐ์รู้ความจริงว่าสุวิญชาถูกใส่ร้ายจึงตามไปหาสุวิญชา
ที่เมืองสิงหลและได้พบกับพระนารายณ์ธิเบศร์ซึ่งกำลังเที่ยวป่ากับพี่เลี้ยง
พระไชยเชษฐ์เห็นพระนารายณ์ธิเบศร์เป็นเด็กน่ารัก มีหน้าตาคล้ายตัวเอง
จึงมั่นใจว่าเป็นลูกชาย พยายามเข้าไปขออุ้มและเอาขนมให้ แต่พระนา
รายณ์ธิเบศร์โกรธพระไชยเชษฐ์ที่จะมาเข้ามาจับตัวเอง จึงใช้ธนูยิงเพื่อ
หวังจะฆ่าให้ตาย แต่ธนูที่ยิงออกไปนั้นกลายเป็นดอกไม้กระจายเต็มพื้น
ดิน จึงทำให้พระไชยเชษฐ์เกิดความประหลาดใจยิ่ง เขาจึงอธิษฐานว่าถ้า
เด็กชายคนนี้เป็นลูกของตนที่เกิดกับสุวิญชา ขอให้ธนูที่ยิงออกไปนั้น
กลายเป็นอาหาร ทันใดนั้นพระไชยเชษฐ์ก็ยิงธนูออกไป และศรธนูนั้นก็
กลายเป็นอาหารมากมายเต็มพื้น จึงทำให้พระไชยเชษฐ์มั่นใจว่าเป็น
ลูกชายของตนจริง

พระไชยเชษฐ์ถามพระนารายณ์ธิเบศร์ถึงแม่ พระนารายณ์ธิเบศร์บอก
ว่าสุวิญชาเป็นแม่และท้าวสิงหลเป็นพ่อ พระไชยเชษฐ์จึงเล่าเรื่องที่ผ่านมา
ให้พระนารายณ์ธิเบศร์ฟัง เขาจึงรู้ว่าเป็นพ่อลูกกัน พระนารายณ์ธิเบศร์
พาพระไชยเชษฐ์ไปพบท้าวสิงหล พระไชยเชษฐ์ขอโทษสุวิญชา ส่วน
ลูกชายก็ช่วยพูดกับสุวิญชาเพื่อให้หายโกรธพ่อ สุวิญชายกโทษให้พระ
ไชยเชษฐ์ ทำให้ทั้งสามคนได้อยู่ด้วยกันเป็นครอบครัวอย่างมีความสุข

Vocabulary

1	ดอกจำปาทอง	dàwk jam paa thawng	golden champak flowers
2	พเนจร	phá neh jawn	to wander
3	โหร	hŏhn	soothsayer
4	สนม	sà-nŏm	concubine
5	หลงทาง	lŏng thaang	to lose one's way
6	ราชการ	ráp râat chá gaan	government official
7	ข้าศึก	khâa sùek	enemy
8	โจมตี	johm tii	to attack
9	อาสา	aa săa	to volunteer
10	ชนะ	chá ná	to defeat, win
11	ชายา	chaa yaa	the wife of a prince
12	อิจฉา	ìt-chăa	jealous
13	คลอดลูก	khlâwt lûuk	to give birth
14	ช้างเผือก	cháang phùeak	white elephant
15	ศร	săwn	bow, arrow
16	พระขรรค์	phrá khăn	dagger
17	ช่วยชีวิต	chûay chii wít	to keep (someone) alive, save (someone's) life
18	ท่อนไม้	thâwn mái	log
19	ใส่ร้าย	sài ráay	to malign
20	พี่เลี้ยง	phîi líang	nursemaid
21	ธนู	thá-nuu	bow
22	ประหลาดใจ	prà-làat jai	to be astonished
23	ยกโทษ	yók thôht	forgiveness

Culture Notes

Hŏhn (soothsayer) refers to a prophet who can predict someone's destiny or determine auspicious times. It is assumed that the term derives from the Thai word for astrologer. In Thai society, people's belief in and practice of astrology began long ago. The stars were consulted to determine auspicious times (for a marriage, opening a new business, etc.), predict future events, identify good or bad omens, or get advice on how to attract luck and avoid misfortune. Since ancient times, Thai kings have had the *horathipdi* (royal astrologer) to advise them about auspicious times for important events.

Comprehension Questions

1. โหรทำนายฝันว่าท้าวสิงหลจะได้อะไร

2. สุวิญชาคลอดลูกเป็นผู้ชายมีอะไรติดตัวมาด้วย

3. นางสนมทั้ง 7 คน ทำอะไรพระไชยเชษฐ์จึงขับไล่สุวิญชาออกจากเมือง

Writing Activity

เลือกสถานการณ์ที่สำคัญที่สุดในเรื่องและเขียนอธิบายว่าทำไมถึงเลือก พร้อมกับยกตัวอย่าง

Pick the most important situation/event in the story and explain why you chose it. Please give examples to support your choice.

Princess Sano-Noi

The king of Romwisai City had a daughter named Sano-Noi Ruean-Ngam ("Sano-Noi of the Lovely House"). She was named thus because at birth she had come into the world with a tiny wooden house clasped in her hands. As she grew older, the house became her most cherished plaything. Miraculously, she was even able to enter the house despite its diminutive size. When Sano-Noi turned 15, the king's soothsayer told him that her fate was to leave the city and travel alone for one year. Although they were reluctant, the king and queen knew they had no choice but to send her away. The next day, they disguised Sano-Noi as a villager and led her to the city gates.

Sano-Noi traveled aimlessly though the forest. Seeing this, the god Indra felt pity for her. He took the form of an ascetic and bestowed upon her a magic potion that could resurrect the dead. Later as she walked deeper into the forest, Sano-Noi came upon a girl with a ghoulish face named Kula. She was sprawled out on the forest floor, having died of a snakebite. Sano-Noi used the ascetic's magic potion to treat the girl's wound, and she

โสนน้อยเรือนงาม

ที่นครโรมวิสัย พระราชามีลูกสาวชื่อ "โสนน้อยเรือนงาม" เพราะเกิดมามี
เรือนไม้เล็กๆ ติดมือออกมาด้วย เมื่อลูกสาวโตขึ้นเรือนไม้นี้จึงกลายเป็น
ของเล่นที่โปรดปรานมาก โสนน้อยสามารถเข้าออกเรือนไม้นั้นได้อย่าง
น่าอัศจรรย์ เมื่อโสนน้อยอายุครบ 15 ปี โหรบอกพระราชาว่าโสนน้อย
กำลังมีเคราะห์ ควรให้ออกจากเมืองแล้วเดินทางเพียงลำพังเป็นเวลา 1 ปี
ถึงแม้พระราชาและพระราชินีจะไม่เห็นด้วยแต่ก็จำใจต้องปฏิบัติตาม ดัง
นั้นในเช้าวันรุ่งขึ้นทั้งสองคนจึงไปส่งลูกสาวที่หน้าประตูเมือง โดยให้โสน
น้อยปลอมตัวเป็นชาวบ้าน

โสนน้อยเดินทางเข้าป่าอย่างไร้จุดหมาย พระอินทร์เกิดความสงสารจึง
แปลงร่างเป็นชีปะขาวมามอบยาวิเศษให้สำหรับรักษาคนตายให้ฟื้นได้
จากนั้นระหว่างทางโสนน้อยพบหญิงสาวหน้าตาน่ากลัวชื่อ "กุลา" นอน
ตายอยู่กลางป่าเพราะถูกงูพิษกัด โสนน้อยจึงลองใช้ยาวิเศษของท่าน

regained consciousness. Kula requested that henceforth she be allowed to accompany Sano-Noi as her servant to wherever her travels may take her.

In the city of Nop-Pharat, the king's once handsome and talented son, Wichit Chinda, had been bitten by a snake and had lost his life seven years prior. The royal soothsayer had predicted that within seven years of the prince's death, a girl from another city would appear and resurrect him. When Sano-Noi and Kula arrived in Nop-Pharat, they overheard an announcement calling for someone to revive a prince who had long been dead. So, they made their way to the palace. Sano-Noi volunteered to treat the prince on the condition she be hidden behind seven layers of curtains, with Kula placed on guard so that no one could see her as she tended his wounds.

Sano-Noi slowly and gingerly applied the magic potion over the prince's entire body until the poison was gradually expelled and became a sweltering vapor that filled the room. Sano-Noi became so hot that she hastily removed her clothing and promptly left to bathe. While she was gone, Kula, who had been harboring feelings of jealousy toward her companion, snatched her abandoned clothing and slipped it on. When the prince awoke, Kula pretended to be the foreign king's daughter who had resurrected him and claimed that Sano-Noi was merely her personal slave. From then on, Sano-Noi was forced to be Kula's servant and was habitually mistreated.

One day, Prince Wichit Chinda became suspicious, as Kula did not behave like the daughter of a king. So, he ordered her to fashion a *krathong* from some banana leaves. Try as she might, Kula could not manage the task, so she hurled the leaves away, scattering them all around. Sano-Noi collected the banana leaves that Kula had discarded and fastened them together into a resplendent *krathong*. Upon seeing this, Kula wrested the piece away from her and brought it to Wichit Chinda. The queen saw it and was satisfied with the elegantly crafted container. She then had Kula dye a multi-colored length of fabric to tie around Prince Wichit Chinda's ship, as he was going out to sea the following day. But Kula found herself once again unable to complete her charge, so she tossed away the fabric and threw out the dye. Sano-Noi retrieved the discarded materials and colored the fabric in exquisite hues. Kula snatched the cloth from her and gave it to the queen as she had done before.

ชีปะขาวรักษาบาดแผล ทำให้กุลาฟื้นขึ้นมา ตั้งแต่นั้นมากุลาจึงขอเป็น
ทาสติดตามโสนน้อยไปทุกที่

ที่เมืองนพรัตน์ กษัตริย์มีลูกชายชื่อ "พระวิจิตรจินดา" เป็นชายหนุ่ม
รูปงามและมีความสามารถ แต่พระวิจิตรจินดาถูกงูพิษกัดตายมานานถึง
7 ปี และโหรทำนายว่าเขาจะฟื้นภายใน 7 ปี เพราะจะมีหญิงสาวจากต่าง
เมืองมาชุบชีวิต เมื่อโสนน้อยและกุลาเดินทางมาถึงเมืองนพรัตน์ได้ยิน
ประกาศว่าต้องการคนมารักษาลูกชายที่ตายไป 7 ปีแล้ว จึงเข้าไปในวัง
และอาสาทำการรักษาพระวิจิตรจินดาให้ฟื้น โดยมีข้อแม้ว่าขอให้กั้นม่าน
เจ็ดชั้น ไม่ให้ใครเห็นเวลารักษาโดยมีกุลาติดตามเฝ้าดู

โสนน้อยค่อย ๆ ทายาวิเศษทั่วร่างกายของพระวิจิตรจินดาอย่าง
เบามือ จนพิษงูค่อย ๆ คายออกมาเป็นไอร้อนไปทั่วห้อง โสนน้อยรู้สึก
ร้อนมากจึงรีบถอดชุดออกแล้วไปอาบน้ำทันที ระหว่างนั้นกุลาซึ่งมีความ
อิจฉาโสนน้อยอยู่แล้วได้นำชุดของโสนน้อยมาใส่ เมื่อพระวิจิตรจินดาฟื้น
ขึ้นมา กุลาก็สวมรอยว่าตัวเองเป็นคนรักษา และเป็นลูกสาวกษัตริย์จาก
ต่างเมือง ส่วนโสนน้อยเป็นทาสผู้ติดตาม ตั้งแต่นั้นมาโสนน้อยจึงตกเป็น
ทาสของกุลาและถูกรังแกอยู่เสมอ

อยู่มาวันหนึ่งพระวิจิตรจินดามีความสงสัยในตัวกุลาว่ากิริยามารยาท
ไม่สมกับเป็นลูกสาวกษัตริย์เลยจึงสั่งให้เย็บกระทงใบตอง แต่กุลา
พยายามทำเท่าไรก็ไม่สำเร็จจึงโยนใบตองทิ้งจนเกลื่อนกลาด โสนน้อยจึง
เก็บใบตองที่ถูกทิ้งนำมาเย็บเป็นกระทงที่สวยงาม กุลาเห็นเข้าก็แย่งนำไป
ให้พระวิจิตรจินดา พระราชินีเห็นกระทงที่เย็บอย่างประณีตและสวยงาม
อย่างพอใจ จึงสั่งให้กุลาย้อมผ้าสามสีสำหรับผูกเรือให้พระวิจิตรจินดา
เพราะจะออกเรือไปทางทะเลในวันรุ่งขึ้น แต่กุลาทำไม่เป็น กลับโยนผ้า
และสีทิ้ง โสนน้อยจึงเก็บผ้าและสีไปย้อมได้สวยงดงาม กุลาก็แย่งนำไป
ให้พระราชินีอีก

When the time came for the prince to set sail, he was unable to free his boat from the harbor. He presumed this was because there was some virtuous person in the palace who wanted something brought back from his trip. So, he ordered one of his soldiers to gather requests from everyone in the palace. But no one had bothered to ask Sano-Noi, so the ship still would not budge. The prince had the soldier return to the palace and search once more. This time, he encountered Sano-Noi, who told him that she wanted a beautiful miniature house. After this, the ship was finally able to clear the harbor.

While the vessel was at sea, the god Indra summoned a wind to steer the ship toward Sano-Noi's home city of Romwisai. The prince had found nearly all of the items that those in the palace had requested. The only thing he had been unable to locate was that for which Sano-Noi had asked. So he asked the townspeople, who informed him that the only place to find such a thing would be in the palace. Prince Wichit Chinda thus made his way to the palace and asked to buy the tiny house to give to a slave girl. Sano-Noi's father, the king, had the prince describe this slave's appearance and knew immediately that she was his daughter. So, he allowed the prince to return with the tiny house in hand.

Once the prince arrived back in Nop-Pharat, one of his soldiers presented the gift to Sano-Noi. She placed the house in front of her and focused her prayers. Suddenly, a radiant light burst from the miniature dwelling and it grew much larger. Sano-Noi then arose and gracefully entered the structure. All who saw this realized that Sano-Noi was someone with great merit and that she was the one who had brought the prince back to life. The prince immediately exiled Kula for her treachery, and from then on, he and Sano-Noi lived happily together.

เมื่อถึงเวลาพระวิจิตรจินดาก็ไม่สามารถเคลื่อนเรือออกจากท่าได้ เขา
คิดว่าคงมีผู้มีบุญในวังต้องการของอะไรบางอย่าง จึงให้ทหารไปถามทุก
คนทั่ววัง แต่ไม่มีใครไปถามโสนน้อย เรือจึงยังเคลื่อนที่ไม่ได้ พระวิจิตร
จินดาให้ทหารกลับไปค้นหาอีกครั้ง จนพบโสนน้อยซึ่งบอกว่าอยากได้
"โสนน้อยเรือนงาม" เพียงเท่านั้นเรือก็เคลื่อนที่ออกจากท่าได้

ขณะที่เรือแล่นไปในทะเล พระอินทร์ก็ดลบันดาลให้ลมพัดเรือไปยัง
นครโรมวิสัยของโสนน้อย พระวิจิตรจินดาหาของได้ตามที่ทุกคนต้องการ
เกือบครบ ขาดแต่เพียงของโสนน้อยเท่านั้นที่หาไม่ได้ พระวิจิตรจินดาจึง
สอบถามจากชาวเมือง ชาวเมืองบอกว่าโสนน้อยเรือนงามมีอยู่แต่ในวัง
เท่านั้น พระวิจิตรจินดาจึงเข้าไปในวังและขอซื้อโสนน้อยเรือนงามไปให้
นางทาส พระราชาซึ่งเป็นพ่อของโสนน้อยถามถึงรูปร่างหน้าตาของนาง
ทาส ก็รู้ว่าเป็นลูกสาว จึงมอบโสนน้อยเรือนงามให้พระวิจิตรจินดา

เมื่อพระวิจิตรจินดาเดินทางกลับถึงเมืองนพรัตน์ ทหารก็ยกเรือนงาม
ไปให้โสนน้อย เมื่อรับเรือนหลังน้อยแล้ววางไว้ตรงหน้า โสนน้อยก็ตั้งจิต
อธิษฐาน ทันใดนั้นก็ปรากฏแสงสว่างเจิดจ้าขึ้นโดยรอบ เรือนหลังน้อยก็
ขยายเป็นเรือนใหญ่ โสนน้อยลุกขึ้นเดินเข้าไปในเรือนนั้นอย่างสง่างาม
ทำให้ทุกคนรู้ว่าแท้จริงแล้วโสนน้อยเป็นผู้มีบุญญาธิการมาก และเป็นผู้ที่
รักษาพระวิจิตรจินดาให้มีชีวิตอีกครั้ง ส่วนกุลาเป็นคนทรยศจึงถูกพระ
วิจิตรจินดาขับไล่ออกจากเมืองทันที นับแต่นั้นมาพระวิจิตรจินดาและโสน
น้อยอยู่ด้วยกันอย่างมีความสุข

Vocabulary

1	เรือนไม้	ruean mái	wooden house
2	ของเล่น	khǎwng lên	toy, plaything
3	น่าอัศจรรย์	nâa àt sà jan	miraculously
4	มีเคราะห์	mii khráw	to be fated to (do/experience something)
5	ปลอมตัว	plawm tua	to disguise
6	ไร้จุดหมาย	rái jùt mǎay	aimless
7	ชีปะขาว	chii-pà-khǎaw	ascetic
8	ยาวิเศษ	yaa wí sèht	magic potion
9	รักษา	rák sǎa	to treat
10	ฟื้น, ชุบชีวิต	fúehn, chûp chii-wít	to resurrect
11	ทาส	thâat	servant, slave
12	สวมรอย	sǔam rawy	to claim
13	รังแก	rang gaeh	to mistreat
14	แย่ง	yâehng	to snatch
15	ผู้มีบุญ	phûu mii bun	virtuous person
16	พระอินทร์	phrá in	Indra (Hindu/Buddhist god)
17	ดลบันดาล	don ban daan	to summon
18	อธิษฐาน	à thít thǎan	to pray
19	บุญญาธิการ	bun yaa thí gaan	great merit
20	ทรยศ	thaw-rá-yót	treachery

Culture Notes

The term "**phûu mii bun**" (virtuous person) is often used to give recognition and respect to people who are successful or have achieved various accomplishments despite obstacles or hardships. They are thought to possess great merit, which is accumulated as a result of good deeds, acts, or thoughts. Having great merit can transform them into strong and courageous people who remain stoic in the face of obstacles or problems because they are confident in their purity. When people who possess great merit decide to do something, their merit fully supports their actions.

Comprehension Questions

1. เมื่อโสนน้อยอายุครบ 15 ปี โหรบอกพระราชาว่าอย่างไร?
2. ทำไมพระวิจิตรจินดาถึงฟื้นจากถูกงูพิษกัดตาย
3. เกิดอะไรขึ้นเมื่อโสนน้อยวางเรือนหลังน้อยไว้ตรงหน้าและตั้งจิตอธิษฐาน

Writing Activity

เขียนหนึ่งย่อหน้าว่าชอบตอนไหนในเรื่องนี้และอธิบายว่าทำไมถึงชอบ

Write a brief paragraph about your favorite part of this story and explain why you like it.

The Story of Phikun Thong

There was once a widow with two daughters; the eldest was named Mali and the youngest Phikun. Phikun was pretty and well-mannered. She was a goodhearted child and always spoke sweetly. However, Mali had always been the favorite, as she most resembled her mother, both in appearance and behavior. Because of this, Phikun was forced to work much harder than her sister, day in and day out.

One day after pounding the rice, Phikun went to fetch some water from the canal near their home. On her way back, she happened to meet an old woman, who asked her if she could spare any water for a drink. Phikun gladly shared some of her water with the woman and bade her to take extra, that she might wash her face and body. She told the woman not to worry, if there was not enough, she could always go back and get more. The old woman smiled and praised Phikun, "Not only are you beautiful, but you have a warm heart as well. Despite my poor and bedraggled appearance, you treat me with kindness." Then, she bestowed upon Phikun a blessing that whenever she spoke, golden *bakula* blossoms would fall from her lips. Once she had conferred the blessing, the woman vanished right before Phikun's eyes.

พิกุลทอง

หญิงหม้ายคนหนึ่งมีลูกสาว 2 คน คนโตชื่อ "มะลิ" คนที่สองชื่อ "พิกุล" พิกุลหน้าตาสวย กิริยามารยาทเรียบร้อย พูดจาไพเราะและน้ำใจงาม แต่แม่ลำเอียงรักมะลิมากกว่าเพราะมีรูปร่างหน้าตาและนิสัยเหมือนแม่ พิกุลจึงต้องทำงานหนักทุกวัน

วันหนึ่งหลังจากตำข้าวเสร็จแล้ว พิกุลก็ออกไปตักน้ำที่ลำธารซึ่งอยู่ไม่ไกลจากบ้าน ระหว่างทางพิกุลพบกับหญิงชราคนหนึ่งมาขอน้ำดื่ม พิกุลแบ่งน้ำไปด้วยความเต็มใจ และยังบอกให้หญิงชราเอาน้ำไปอีกเพื่อจะได้ล้างหน้าและล้างตัวให้สดชื่น พิกุลบอกว่าไม่ต้องห่วงเพราะถ้าน้ำไม่พอจะไปตักมาอีก หญิงชรายิ้มและพูดชมพิกุลว่า "นอกจากจะสวยแล้วยังใจดีอีก ถึงฉันจะดูยากจนและมอมแมม แต่ก็ปฏิบัติกับฉันเป็นอย่างดี" หลังจากนั้นหญิงชราก็ให้พรวิเศษกับพิกุล เมื่อไรก็ตามที่พิกุลพูดออกมา จะมีดอกพิกุลทองร่วงออกมาจากปากเสมอ หลังจากหญิงชราให้พรวิเศษแล้วก็หายวับไปต่อหน้าต่อตา

Immediately upon arriving home, Phikun's mother rebuked her for dawdling and trying to skirt her duties. So, Phikun recounted all that had happened. As she did so, golden *bakula* blossoms flitted down out of her mouth. Her mother's anger instantly morphed into greed and she rushed to collect all of the golden blossoms, ordering Phikun to carry on speaking that she might sate her own desire. After that day, her mother would collect as many of Phikun's golden blossoms as she could, which she would then take and exchange for money.

The family's livelihood improved and Phikun no longer had to work as hard as before. However, she was forced to speak all day so as to produce as many of the golden blossoms as possible. She eventually became weary. Her throat grew sore and her voice hoarse until she could no longer speak. This enraged her mother to the point where she would beat Phikun to force more words from her mouth. But soon Phikun was no longer able to utter even a single syllable.

Her mother then had an idea. She sent Mali to fetch water as Phikun had done in the hope that Mali might also encounter the elderly woman. But rather than an old woman, Mali came upon a beautiful girl dressed in elegant clothing standing in the shade of a tree. The girl asked Mali for water, but Mali snapped back in refusal, both because she was jealous of the girl's appearance and because she did not think that this child could be the fairy her sister had encountered. But in truth, the girl was a tree spirit, who then placed a curse on Mali that whenever she spoke in anger, maggots, worms, and millipedes would fall from her lips.

When Mali returned home, she furiously described to her mother what had taken place. With each word, maggots, worms, and millipedes tumbled out of her mouth, filling the house. Their mother surmised that a jealous Phikun must have twisted the events in her story so as to prevent Mali from meeting the old woman, so she beat her and threw her out of the house.

After leaving her mother's house, Phikun went alone into the woods. A prince was riding by on his horse when he noticed her crouched there on the ground, sobbing. He asked of her troubles, and Phikun told him all that had happened. When she had finished speaking, the ground around her was blanketed in golden blossoms. The prince was overjoyed, as he realized that this girl must be his soulmate. He had had a dream the previous night

ทันทีที่กลับถึงบ้านช้า พิกุลก็ถูกแม่ดุด่าว่าเถลไถลหนีงาน ดังนั้นพิกุล
จึงเล่าเรื่องทั้งหมดให้แม่ฟัง ขณะที่เล่าก็มีดอกพิกุลทองร่วงออกมาจาก
ปากด้วย แม่ก็เปลี่ยนอารมณ์จากโกรธเป็นละโมบในทันที รีบเก็บดอก
พิกุลทองทั้งหมดพร้อมกับสั่งให้พิกุลพูดต่อไปเรื่อย ๆ เพื่อสนองความ
ละโมบของตัวเอง นับจากวันนั้นเป็นต้นมาแม่เก็บรวบรวมดอกพิกุลทอง
ไว้ให้มากที่สุดเท่าที่จะทำได้เพื่อนำไปขายแลกเงินมา

ครอบครัวตอนนี้มีความเป็นอยู่ที่ดีขึ้น พิกุลเองไม่ต้องทำงานหนัก
เหมือนแต่ก่อน แต่ก็ถูกบังคับให้พูดทั้งวันเพื่อให้ดอกพิกุลทองร่วงออก
มาจากปากครั้งละมาก ๆ พิกุลเริ่มอ่อนล้า มีอาการเจ็บคอและเสียงแหบ
จนพูดไม่ได้ ทำให้แม่โมโหมากถึงขั้นตบตีพิกุลเพื่อบังคับให้พูด แต่พิกุลก็
พูดไม่ได้แม้แต่คำเดียว

แม่จึงเกิดความคิดส่งมะลิเดินไปตักน้ำอย่างที่ทำพิกุลเคยทำ แต่แทนที่
มะลิจะได้พบกับหญิงชรากลับเป็นหญิงสาวสวยแต่งตัวสวยงามยืนอยู่ใต้
ร่มไม้ หญิงสาวคนนั้นขอน้ำจากมะลิ แต่มะลิปฏิเสธไม่ให้น้ำและยังพูด
หยาบคายเพราะอิจฉาที่หญิงสาวสวยกว่าตัวเองและคิดว่าหญิงคนนั้น
ไม่ใช่นางฟ้า แต่ความจริงแล้วหญิงสาวคือนางไม้ นางไม้จึงสาปแช่งมะลิ
ว่า เมื่อไรก็ตามที่มะลิโกรธและพูดออกมาก็จะมีหนอน ไส้เดือน กิ้งกือ
ร่วงออกมาจากปาก

เมื่อกลับมาถึงบ้านมะลิก็เล่าเรื่องทั้งหมดให้แม่ฟังด้วยความโกรธ เมื่อ
มะลิพูดคำไหนออกมาก็จะมีหนอน ไส้เดือน กิ้งกือ ร่วงลงมาจากปากจน
เต็มบ้านไปหมด แม่คิดว่าพิกุลอิจฉามะลิที่บิดเบือนไม่เล่าเรื่องจริงทั้งหมด
ทำให้มะลิไม่ได้พบกับหญิงชรา แม่จึงทุบตีพิกุลและไล่ออกจากบ้านไป

เมื่อออกจากบ้านพิกุลก็เดินเข้าไปในป่าเพียงลำพัง ขณะนั้นเองมีเจ้า
ชายขี่ม้าผ่านมาเห็นพิกุลนั่งร้องไห้อยู่จึงเข้าไปถาม พิกุลเล่าเรื่องทั้งหมด
ให้ฟัง ทันทีที่พูดจบพื้นที่บริเวณนั้นก็เต็มไปด้วยดอกพิกุลทอง เจ้าชาย
ดีใจและรู้ว่าพิกุลคือเนื้อคู่ เพราะเมื่อคืนฝันว่าเดินผ่านต้นไม้ใหญ่และพบ

that he had met an old woman by a large tree. She had told him to go riding into the forest the following day and that there he would encounter his true love—a girl who produced golden *bakula* blossoms when she spoke.

The prince asked Phikun for her hand in marriage. The two of them then bowed before a large tree and prayed for the spirit's blessing and that they would be happy thereafter.

Vocabulary

1	หม้าย	**mâay**	widow
2	นิสัย	**ní-săi**	behavior
3	ลำเอียง	**lam iang**	to be partial, play favorites
4	ด้วยความเต็มใจ	**dûay khwaam tem jai**	gladly
5	พรวิเศษ	**phawn wí sèht**	blessing
6	ดอกพิกุลทอง	**dàwk phí gun thawng**	golden *bakula* blossoms
7	ร่วง	**rûang**	to fall
8	หายวับ	**hăay wáp**	to vanish
9	เถลไถล	**thà lĕh thà lăi**	to dawdle
10	ละโมบ	**lá môhp**	greed
11	เก็บ	**gèp**	to collect
12	บังคับ	**bang kháp**	to force
13	อ่อนล้า	**àwn láa**	weary
14	เสียงแหบ	**sĭang hàehp**	hoarse (voice)
15	นางฟ้า	**naang fáa**	fairy
16	นางไม้	**naang mái**	tree spirit
17	สาปแช่ง	**sàap châehng**	curse
18	หนอน	**năwn**	maggot
19	ไส้เดือน	**sâi duean**	worm
20	กิ้งกือ	**gîng gueh**	millipede
21	บิดเบือน	**bìt buean**	to twist

กับหญิงชราคนหนึ่งบอกว่าให้ขี่ม้าเข้ามาในป่าวันนี้แล้วจะได้พบเนื้อคู่เป็น
หญิงที่มีดอกพิกุลทองร่วงเมื่อพูดออกมา

เจ้าชายจึงขอพิกุลแต่งงาน จากนั้นเจ้าชายก็พาพิกุลไปกราบต้นไม้ใหญ่
เพื่อขอพรจากนางไม้ให้ทั้งสองคนมีความสุขตลอดไป

22	เจ้าชาย	**jâo-chaay**	prince
23	เนื้อคู่	**núea khûu**	soulmate

Culture Notes

The Thai proverb, "Fearing that *bakula* blossoms will fall from one's mouth" comes from this fable. It is often used in a sarcastic way to refer to a quiet person who does not dare to speak out. An example might go something like this: "You are not answering any of my questions. Are you afraid that *bakula* flowers are going to fall out of your mouth?" This fable must have been very popular for it to have coined a proverb that is still widely used by Thai people today!

Comprehension Questions

1. ทำไมแม่รักมะลิมากกว่าพิกุล
2. หญิงชราให้พรวิเศษอะไรกับพิกุล
3. เมื่อมะลิโกรธและพูดออกมาจะมีอะไรร่วงออกมาจากปาก

Writing Activity

สมมติว่าคุณกำลังสัมภาษณ์ตัวละครคนหนึ่งในนิทานเรื่องนี้ เขียนคำถาม
และคำตอบของตัวละคร

Imagine you were going to interview a character in the story. List the questions you would ask, and the possible answers given by that character.

The Twelve Sisters (Nang Sip Song)

There was once a wealthy couple who had long been married, but who were unable to have children. They prayed to the spirits, and not long after, the wife became pregnant and gave birth to twelve girls. As the girls became older, the once-wealthy family sank into poverty. The husband thus attempted to trick the girls and abandon them in the woods. However, Phao, the youngest of the girls—also the prettiest and cleverest—was able to lead her sisters safely back to their house. But their parents were persistent and tried once again to abandon them in the forest, this time succeeding in doing so.

An ogress named Santra was journeying through the woods when she spied the twelve sisters sleeping. Out of compassion, she decided to take them in and raise them as her own, ordering everyone in her city to take human form until the girls had grown up so as not to frighten them. One day, the sisters discovered a mountain of bones hidden in a tunnel, and this alerted them to Santra's secret. Overcome with terror, the girls decided to sneak out of the city.

นางสิบสอง

เศรษฐีสองสามีภรรยาแต่งงานกันมานานแต่ไม่มีลูก จึงได้บนบานขอลูก
กับเทวดา ต่อมาไม่นานภรรยาก็ตั้งท้องแล้วคลอดลูกสาวออกมา 12 คน
เมื่อลูกสาวทั้ง 12 คน โตขึ้น ครอบครัวของเขาจากฐานะที่เคยร่ำรวยก็เริ่ม
จนลงเรื่อยๆ สามีจึงต้องใช้อุบายเอาลูกไปปล่อยไว้ในป่า ในบรรดาลูกสาว
สิบสองคนมีลูกคนสุดท้องชื่อ "เภา" ที่มีหน้าตางดงามและฉลาดกว่าพี่
สาวทุกคน สามารถพาพี่สาวกลับบ้านได้อย่างปลอดภัย แต่พ่อแม่ก็ไม่ลด
ความพยายามนำลูกสาวไปปล่อยอีกครั้งซึ่งครั้งนี้ก็สำเร็จ

  ขณะที่รอนแรมอยู่ในป่า นางยักษ์ชื่อ "สารตรา" เห็นเด็กสาวทั้งสิบ
สองคนนอนหลับอยู่เกิดรักและเอ็นดูจึงนำไปเลี้ยงเป็นลูก และสั่งให้
คนในเมืองแปลงกายเป็นมนุษย์เพื่อไม่ให้เด็กทั้งสิบสองกลัวจนกระทั่ง
เติบโตเป็นสาว วันหนึ่งนางสิบสองรู้ความลับว่านางสารตราเป็นยักษ์
เพราะไปพบกองกระดูกมากมายอยู่ในอุโมงค์ นางสิบสองเกิดความหวาด
กลัวจึงพยายามหลบหนีออกมาจากเมือง

Just then, the king Rot-Thasit was out on a stroll in the woods, and he came upon the twelve sisters. He was pleased by their beauty and brought them back to his palace, where he married all of them, making them his queens. Soon after, all twelve sisters simultaneously became pregnant. Meanwhile, the ogress Santra was furious at the girls' desertion. So she cast a spell to find them and devised a trick that would allow her to get her revenge.

Santra transformed into a beautiful young woman and traveled to the palace to meet King Rot-Thasit. She then cast a spell on the king, that he be enamored with her and detest the twelve sisters. Under the ogress's spell, the king ordered his wives to be imprisoned in a cave. In her great resentment, Santra then feigned illness and told the king that only medicine derived from the eyes of the twelve sisters would cure her. His infatuation with the ogress caused him to fall for the ruse and order his wives seized from the cave and their eyes gouged out. But the youngest, Phao, had only one removed so that she may see the world through her remaining eye. Subsequently, all twelve sisters gave birth in the cave, but eleven of the infants died, devoured by their starving mothers. Only Phao's child, Rot-Thasen, survived, as Phao alone had refused to consume her sisters' children. Rot-Thasen was a dutiful child and would often slip out of the cave to find food for his mother and aunts.

Rot-Thasen grew into a handsome young man full of intelligence and gratitude. He raised roosters and would enter them in the villagers' cockfights. Whenever he won, he would request food to bring to his mother and aunts. Because of this, he became well known throughout the land. King Rot-Thasit heard about a young man who was good looking and quite unlike the other villagers. He wondered about this boy and summoned him. And upon meeting him, the king realized that Rot-Thasen was his and Phao's son.

ในขณะนั้นเป็นเวลาเดียวกับที่ท้าวรถสิทธิ์เดินเที่ยวอยู่ในป่าและได้พบ
นางสิบสอง เขาเกิดความพึงพอใจในความงามของนางทั้งสิบสองคนจึงพา
เข้าวังแต่งตั้งให้ทุกคนเป็นมเหสี และนางสิบสองก็ตั้งครรภ์พร้อมกันฝ่าย
นางยักษ์สารตราโกรธแค้นที่นางสิบสองหนี จึงใช้เวทมนต์ตามหาจนเจอ
และคิดอุบายเพื่อแก้แค้นทั้งสิบสองคน

นางยักษ์สารตราได้แปลงกายเป็นสาวงามเข้ามาพบท้าวรถสิทธิ์ในวัง
และร่ายมนต์ให้ท้าวรถสิทธิ์เกิดความลุ่มหลงตัวเองและเกลียดชังนางสิบ
สองพร้อมกับสั่งให้จับนางสิบสองไปขังไว้ในถ้ำ ด้วยความเคียดแค้นนาง
สิบสองเป็นอย่างยิ่ง นางยักษ์สารตราแกล้งล้มป่วยและใช้อุบายบอกกับ
ท้าวรถสิทธิ์ว่าจำเป็นต้องใช้ดวงตาทั้งสิบสองคนมาเป็นยารักษาโรคจึงจะ
หาย ท้าวรถสิทธิ์ซึ่งกำลังลุ่มหลงอยู่ก็เชื่อจึงสั่งให้จับตัวนางสิบสองไปไว้
ในถ้ำแล้วควักลูกตาออก แต่เภาน้องคนสุดท้องถูกควักตาออกแค่ข้าง
เดียว เพื่อให้เภาได้มีโอกาสเห็นโลกด้วยตาอีกข้างหนึ่ง ต่อมาทั้งสิบสอง
คนคลอดลูกในถ้ำ แต่ลูกของ 11 คน ตายกันหมดเพราะด้วยความหิวจึง
ต้องกินลูกของตัวเอง เหลือเพียงลูกของเภาชื่อ "รถเสน" ที่รอดชีวิต เพ
ราะเภาไม่เคยยอมกินลูกของพี่สาวทุกคนเลย รถเสนเป็นเด็กดีและมัก
หลบหนีออกจากถ้ำเพื่อหาอาหารไปให้แม่และป้ากิน

เมื่อรถเสนเติบโตเป็นชายหนุ่มรูปงาม มีความกตัญญูและมีสติปัญญา
เป็นเลิศ เขาเลี้ยงไก่และนำไก่มาชนกับชาวบ้าน เมื่อได้ชัยชนะจะขออาหาร
มาให้แม่และป้าทุกครั้งจนมีชื่อเสียงเลื่องลือไปทั่ว ท้าวรถสิทธิ์ได้ยินว่ามี
เด็กหนุ่มหน้าตาดีมีลักษณะไม่เหมือนคนอื่น จึงเริ่มสงสัยและเรียกให้
มาพบ ทำให้ได้รู้ความจริงว่ารถเสนคือลูกชายของตัวเองที่เกิดกับเภา

When the ogress-in-disguise, Santra, found out that Rot-Thasen was Phao's child, she once again pretended to be ill and implored the boy to travel to Thantawan City, which was actually a city of ogres, to procure for her some herbs to distill into medicine. She had Rot-Thasen take with him a letter, which he was forbidden to open, to give to her daughter, Meri. In the letter, the ogress had written, "If he arrives in daylight, kill him in daylight. If he arrives at night, kill him at night." However, along the way, Rot-Thasen stopped to rest in a hermit's pavilion in the forest. The hermit sensed what was happening, so he secretly changed the message in the letter to read, "If he arrives in daylight, *marry him* in daylight. If he arrives at night, *marry him* at night." So, when Meri read the letter, she obeyed what she thought were her mother's instructions and married Rot-Thasen, who would henceforth rule over the city.

Rot-Thasen was happy in the city of the ogres, but he missed his mother and aunts. So, he devised a plan to return their eyes to them. One night, he got Meri so drunk that she passed out. He then snatched the satchel containing the sisters' eyes and fled the city. He brought the eyes back to the cave along with a potion that would restore their sight.

This infuriated Santra, who transformed back into an ogre with the intention of killing Rot-Thasen. But he was able to strike at her weak point and slay her. In the end, King Rot-Thasit and the twelve sisters were able to live their lives happily together.

เมื่อนางยักษ์สารตราที่แปลงกายเป็นสาวงามรู้ว่ารถเสนเป็นลูกของ
เภา จึงออกอุบายว่าตัวเองป่วย ขอร้องให้รถเสนเดินทางไปยังเมือง
ทานตะวันซึ่งความจริงคือเมืองยักษ์ เพื่อนำสมุนไพรมาทำยารักษาโรค
และให้รถเสนนำจดหมายไปให้ "เมรี" ซึ่งเป็นลูกสาวด้วยโดยห้ามเปิด
อ่าน นางยักษ์สารตราเขียนข้อความในจดหมายสั่งเมรีว่า "ถึงกลางวันให้
ฆ่ากลางวัน ถึงกลางคืนให้ฆ่ากลางคืน" แต่ระหว่างทางรถเสนหยุดนอน
พักที่ศาลาของพระฤๅษีในป่า พระฤๅษีมีญาณพิเศษเห็นเหตุการณ์จึงแอบ
แก้ข้อความในจดหมายว่า "ถึงกลางวันให้แต่งกลางวัน ถึงกลางคืนให้
แต่งกลางคืน" ดังนั้นเมื่อเมรีอ่านจดหมายแล้ว จึงทำตามคำสั่งแม่ คือ
แต่งงานกับรถเสนและให้ปกครองเมือง

รถเสนอยู่ในเมืองยักษ์ด้วยความสุข แต่ก็ยังคิดถึงแม่และป้าจึงคิดหา
อุบายนำดวงตาของนางสิบสองกลับคืน เขาวางแผนมอมเหล้าเมรีจน
กระทั่งมึนเมาไม่ได้สติ พระรถเสนจึงไปขโมยห่อดวงตาและหนีออกจาก
เมืองไป รถเสนได้นำดวงตากลับมาให้นางสิบสองได้สำเร็จพร้อมกับยา
รักษาจนสามารถมองเห็นได้

นางยักษ์สารตราโกรธมากจึงแปลงกายเป็นยักษ์หวังจะฆ่ารถเสน แต่
เขาสามารถทำลายกล่องดวงใจของนางยักษ์ทำให้นางยักษ์สิ้นใจตาย ใน
ที่สุดท้าวรถสิทธิ์กับนางสิบสองคนก็ใช้ชีวิตอยู่ด้วยกันอย่างมีความสุข

Vocabulary

1	เทวดา	theh-wá-daa	spirit
2	ร่ำรวย	râm ruay	wealthy
3	พยายาม	phá yaa yaam	to try
4	รอนแรม	rawn raehm	to journey
5	มนุษย์	má-nút	human
6	ความลับ	khwaam láp	secret
7	กระดูก	grà dùuk	bone
8	อุโมงค์	ù-mohng	tunnel
9	เวทมนต์	wêht mon	spell
10	แก้แค้น	gâeh kháehn	to take/get revenge
11	ลุ่มหลง	lûm lŏng	to be enamored
12	ความเคียดแค้น	khwaam khîat kháehn	resentment
13	ดวงตา	duang-taa	eye
14	ควัก	khwák	to gouge out
15	รอดชีวิต	râwt chii-wít	to survive
16	กตัญญ	gà-tan-yuu	gratitude
17	สติปัญญา	sà-tì pan-yaa	intelligence
18	ยารักษาโรค	yaa rák săa rôhk	medicine
19	จดหมาย	jòt măay	letter
20	ข้อความ	khâw-khwaam	message
21	ฆ่า	khâa	to kill
22	ญาณ	yaan	sense, perception
23	มอมเหล้า	mawm lâo	to get someone drunk

Culture Notes

In Thai folklore and religious texts, an ogre/ogress or giant/giantess is a type of huge inhuman being who likes raw meat. Influenced by Brahmanism and Buddhism, Thai people believe that there are different types of giants/ogres who differ in their levels of merit. The **high-level giant** (Yák Chán Sǔung) has a golden *vimana* (tallest structure of a temple), a beautiful body, a ring made of pure light, and skin that is greenish black, yellowish or scarlet, and ambrosia. He has servants ready to serve him and his fangs only become visible when he gets angry. The **mid-level giant** (Yák Chán Glaang) mostly serves the high-level giant. The **low-level giant** (Yák Chán Tàm), who possesses little merit, is ugly and mean spirited, with a black body, curly hair, protruding eyes, and rough skin. The giants reside in caves, on mountains, and in the water, soil, and air. They became giants because they made merit with anger in their hearts and were often bad tempered.

Comprehension Questions

1. เพราะอะไรเศรษฐีจึงนำลูกทั้งสิบสองคนไปปล่อยไว้ในป่า

2. นางสิบสองรู้ความลับว่านางสารตราเป็นยักษ์ได้อย่างไร

3. ใครแอบแก้ข้อความในจดหมายว่า "ถึงกลางวันให้แต่งกลางวัน ถึงกลางคืนให้แต่งกลางคืน"

Writing Activity

เขียนตอนจบของเรื่องใหม่ที่สร้างความตื่นเต้นให้มากที่สุด (เท่าที่ทำได้)

Write a different ending to the story. Try to make it as exciting as you can!

The Myth of Phra Ruang

King Uthairaat of the city of Inthapat had a consort named Queen Naak, who had been born into the lineage of Phaya Naga. One day, the king took the queen, who was about to give birth, to the city of Ammara Phirunboon. As day broke, the queen gave birth to a single egg, as befitting her lineage. However, the king, who was unaware of his queen's heritage, thought the egg inauspicious and feared that it may bring misfortune to his city. So, he ordered her to destroy it. But as a mother, the queen could not bear to harm her own child. Before returning to Inthapat, she ordered her confidant to surreptitiously bury the egg along the beach in the hope that some fortuitous person might happen upon it and choose to raise it.

พระร่วงวาจาสิทธิ์

พระเจ้าอุทัยราชเจ้าเมืองอินทปัตมีพระมเหสีชื่อพระนางนาคที่มีชาติกำเนิด
เกิดจากเชื้อสายพญานาค วันหนึ่งพระเจ้าอุทัยราชพาพระนางนาคเดินทาง
ไปเมืองอัมราพิรุณบูรณ์ซึ่งกำลังตั้งครรภ์ใกล้คลอดแล้ว เมื่อถึงเวลาใกล้
รุ่งพระนางนาคก็คลอดลูกออกมาเป็นไข่ 1 ฟอง ตามเชื้อสายนาคที่
สืบทอดกันมา แต่พระเจ้าอุทัยราชไม่เคยรู้ชาติกำเนิดเดิมของพระนางนาค
เกรงว่าไข่ฟองนี้อาจจะเป็นเสนียดจัญไรและทำให้เกิดความอัปมงคลกับ
บ้านเมือง จึงสั่งให้ทำลายไข่ แต่ด้วยความเป็นแม่ไม่อาจทำร้ายลูกได้
ก่อนกลับเมืองอินทปัตพระนางนาคจึงสั่งให้คนสนิทแอบนำไข่ไปฝังไว้ที่
หาดทรายเพื่อรอคนที่มีบุญวาสนามาพบและนำไปชุบเลี้ยง

Some time later, a captain from the city of Lavo (present-day Lopburi) named Khong Khrao was passing by Ammara Phirunboon with his caravan and noticed a peculiarly large egg protruding from the sand. So, Khong Khrao took the egg with him back to Lavo, where he sought a hen to help hatch it. After 10 months had passed, the egg finally cracked open, revealing an adorable baby boy. Khong Khrao named the boy "Ruang" and raised him lovingly as though he were his own son.

Ruang lived a normal childhood, and it was not until his 11th year that he discovered his gift of "sacred speech." One day, he took his boat out on the Chup Son Sea, the source of Lavo's renowned sacred water. He had paddled with the current for a time, which meant that on the way back he was forced to fight the tide. He soon became tired and absent-mindedly said aloud, "Why does the water not flow toward my home?" Instantly, the current shifted direction and carried the boat back to shore. Ruang kept what had happened that day secret, resolving never to let anyone know.

At that time, Lavo was under Khmer rule, and it was Khong Khrao's duty to send sacred water from the Chup Son Sea every three years as tribute to king Suryavarman II, the ruler of the Khmer empire. When Khong Khrao eventually passed away, it fell upon Ruang to take over his duties. When it came time to pay tribute, the Khmer king dispatched an official with 50 wagons and an army of 1,000 soldiers to transport the sacred water from the Chup Son Sea for ceremonial use.

When a commissioner from the Khmer empire heard news of Khong Khrao's death, he sent an official to summon Ruang, who had taken up his adoptive father's duties. Ruang proposed to the official that they use a different kind of container to deliver their tribute. "Bringing cumbersome clay jars to fill with water only adds needless weight. We should work together to weave bamboo baskets to carry our tribute instead. I will order the water not to flow out." The attending soldiers were confounded by the idea of carrying water in baskets full of holes. Ruang was obstinate, "The water will absolutely not leak out." Hearing Ruang's steadfast assurance, the official ordered his soldiers to weave 25 bamboo baskets for each wagon. Should this prove possible, it would allow them to carry nearly double the usual amount, and the more water they were able to convey, the greater favor they would receive from the king.

ในเวลาต่อมาขบวนเกวียนของนายคงเคราซึ่งเป็นนายกองส่งน้ำแห่ง
เมืองละโว้ (จังหวัดลพบุรีในปัจจุบัน) เดินทางผ่านเมืองอัมราพิรุณบูรณ์
ได้พบไข่ 1 ฟองมีขนาดใหญ่กว่าไข่ทั่วไปผุดขึ้นมาบนหาดทราย นายคง
เคราจึงเก็บเอาไปยังเมืองละโว้ด้วย แล้วหาแม่ไก่มาช่วยฟักไข่ เมื่อครบสิบ
เดือนไข่นั้นก็แตกออกปรากฏเป็นเด็กผู้ชายหน้าตาน่ารักน่าเอ็นดู นายคง
เคราตั้งชื่อว่า "ร่วง" และเลี้ยงดูเสมือนลูกด้วยความรักใคร่ตั้งแต่นั้นมา

เด็กชาย "ร่วง" ใช้ชีวิตแบบเด็กคนธรรมดาคนหนึ่ง จนเมื่ออายุได้ 11
ปี เขาจึงรู้เป็นครั้งแรกว่าตัวเองมี "วาจาสิทธิ์" ด้วยเหตุที่วันหนึ่งเขาไป
พายเรือเล่นในทะเลชุบศรต้นกำเนิดแห่งน้ำศักดิ์สิทธิ์ของเมืองละโว้ เขา
พายเรือตามน้ำไปได้สักพัก แต่ขากลับต้องพายเรือทวนน้ำ รู้สึกเหนื่อยจึง
พูดลอย ๆ ออกมาว่า "ทำไมน้ำไม่ไหลกลับไปทางบ้านเราบ้าง" ทันใดนั้น
กระแสน้ำเปลี่ยนทิศทันทีพาเรือไหลกลับไปทางที่เขาพูด ร่วงได้เก็บเรื่อง
นี้ไว้เป็นความลับไม่ให้ใครรู้

ขณะนั้นเมืองละโว้อยู่ในความปกครองของพวกขอม โดยนายคงเครา
มีหน้าที่ต้องส่งส่วยคือ น้ำศักดิ์สิทธิ์จากทะเลชุบศร เป็นประจำทุก 3 ปี
เพื่อไปถวายพระเจ้าสุริยวรมันที่ 2 เจ้าเมืองขอม หลายปีต่อนายคงเครา
เสียชีวิต ร่วงจึงขึ้นมาทำหน้าที่แทน เมื่อถึงกำหนดส่งส่วย เจ้าเมืองขอม
จึงส่งข้าหลวงพร้อมกองเกวียน 50 เล่ม และไพร่พลทหารอีก 1,000 คน
มาบรรทุกน้ำศักดิ์สิทธิ์จากทะเลชุบศร เพื่อนำไปประกอบพิธี

เมื่อข้าหลวงเมืองขอมรู้ข่าวนายคงเคราเสียชีวิตแล้ว จึงให้คนไปตาม
ร่วงซึ่งทำหน้าที่แทนมาพบ ร่วงเสนอความคิดกับข้าหลวงให้เปลี่ยนภา
ชนะใส่น้ำว่า "ท่านเอาโอ่งไหที่ทำด้วยดินมาใส่น้ำอย่างนี้หนักเปล่าๆ จง
ช่วยกันสานชะลอมใส่น้ำ แล้วเราจะสั่งน้ำไม่ให้ไหลออกมาเอง" ไพร่พล
ขอมที่มาด้วยต่างแปลกใจมากว่า ชะลอมที่มีรูจะขนน้ำได้อย่างไร ร่วง
ยืนยันขันแข็งว่า "น้ำไม่รั่วแน่นอน" ข้าหลวงเห็นร่วงรับรองแข็งขันว่า
สามารถทำได้ จึงสั่งให้ไพร่พลสานชะลอมจำนวน 25 ใบ ต่อหนึ่งเกวียน
เพราะถ้าทำได้จริงเท่ากับขนน้ำได้มากกว่าเดิมเกือบสองเท่า ยิ่งขนน้ำได้
มาก ยิ่งได้ความดีความชอบจากเจ้าเมืองขอมมากขึ้น

When it came time to pour the seawater into the baskets, Ruang said simply, "May the water not flow out." And so it was. When all had been filled and placed atop the wagons, it was clear that not a single container had leaked. The Khmer official was simultaneously delighted and astonished. He ordered the water to be loaded into the carts for immediate departure. When they first made camp, the official began to suspect that this might be some kind of ruse. So, he opened the baskets to examine their contents. They were all, indeed, filled with water, and this served as a strong reminder of Ruang's ability.

After they arrived in Khmer, word of the official who had come bearing water in bamboo baskets spread among the citizens. When this reached the king's ear, he summoned the man for questioning. The official told the king in great detail of everything that had happened. He then lifted a basket and poured out some water onto the ground for the king and all of his courtiers to see for themselves. The king surmised that this Ruang must be a person of innate merit and was fearful of any future danger the boy might pose to the Khmer empire. So, he resolved to send a company of soldiers to capture and kill him.

When Ruang heard the news that Khmer soldiers were on their way to kill him, he quickly fled north from Lavo to the city of Phichit, where he sought refuge in a local temple. Out of hunger, he was forced to beg the villagers for food. Once he received a fish. After having eaten all but its bones, he cast the remains into the river and said, "May you have life." The fish reanimated and began swimming around in the water. Ruang wandered for many years, evading Khmer soldiers, until he was old enough to become ordained. From then, he lived as a monk in a temple in the city of Sukhothai, and the villagers called him by the name "Phra Ruang."

เมื่อถึงเวลาเทน้ำใส่ชะลอม ร่วงแค่พูดว่า "ขออย่าให้น้ำรั่วออกมา" เพียงเท่านั้นน้ำก็ไม่รั่ว พอนำชะลอมทุกใบไปตักน้ำตั้งบนเกวียนปรากฏว่าไม่มีน้ำไหลรั่วออกมาเลยแม้แต่ใบเดียว ข้าหลวงเมืองขอมดีใจพร้อมกับแปลกประหลาดใจอย่างมาก จึงสั่งให้รีบขนน้ำขึ้นเกวียนเพื่อเร่งออกเดินทางกลับ เมื่อเดินทางถึงจุดพักที่หนึ่ง ข้าหลวงเกิดเอะใจสงสัยว่าเป็นกลลวงหรือเปล่า จึงเปิดชะลอมเพื่อตรวจดู ปรากฏว่ายังมีน้ำอยู่จริงทุกชะลอม จึงเป็นการตอกย้ำความสามารถของนายร่วงเข้าไปอีก

เมื่อเดินทางมาถึงเมืองขอม ชาวเมืองต่างพากันก็เล่าลือเรื่องที่ข้าหลวงนำชะลอมใส่น้ำบรรทุกมา เจ้าเมืองขอมได้ยินข่าวจึงเรียกข้าหลวงไปสอบถาม เขาจึงเล่าเรื่องราวทั้งหมดให้ฟังอย่างละเอียด พร้อมทั้งยกชะลอมที่ยังมีน้ำขังอยู่เทลงพื้นให้เห็นเจ้าเมืองและเหล่าข้าราชบริพารเห็นกันทั่วหน้า เจ้าเมืองขอมคิดว่าร่วงคือผู้มีบุญมาเกิดและเกรงว่าในอนาคตอาจเป็นอันตรายแก่เมืองขอม จึงสั่งให้ส่งกองทัพทหารไปจับตัวร่วงมาฆ่าให้ตายเสียดีกว่า

เมื่อร่วงรู้ข่าวทหารขอมจะมาจับตัวไปฆ่า เขาจึงรีบหนีออกจากเมืองละโว้ขึ้นไปทางเหนือและหลบอยู่ในวัดแห่งหนึ่งในเขตเมืองพิจิตร ด้วยความอดอยากต้องขออาหารจากชาวบ้านกิน ครั้งหนึ่งร่วงได้ปลามาหนึ่งตัว หลังจากกินปลาหมดเหลือแต่ก้าง เขาก็โยนก้างปลานั้นลงไปในแม่น้ำแล้วพูดว่า "เจ้าจงมีชีวิตขึ้นมาเถิด" แล้วปลาก็กลับมีชีวิตขึ้นมาว่ายน้ำได้เหมือนเดิม ร่วงเพเนจรหลบหนีพวกทหารขอมอยู่เป็นเวลาหลายปี จนเมื่ออายุครบบวชจึงบวชเป็นพระภิกษุอยู่ที่วัดแห่งหนึ่งในเมืองสุโขทัย ชาวบ้านจึงเรียกเขาว่า พระร่วง นับแต่นั้นมา

When a Khmer soldier came upon a clue as to Phra Ruang's whereabouts, he reported to the king and volunteered to find and kill the fugitive. This soldier was skilled in incantations and had the ability to dive beneath the ground. So, he used his power to pass under Sukhothai's outer walls, reappearing at the temple where Phra Ruang resided. The soldier saw Phra Ruang sweeping the temple grounds. But he did not know him by sight and so inquired, "Where can I find Phra Ruang of Lavo City?" Phra Ruang immediately grasped the danger he was in. So, he told the soldier, "You stay here. Do not go anywhere. I will find Phra Ruang." And by the power of his sacred speech, the soldier' body, still half beneath the earth, immediately hardened there and became stone.

Some years later, the ruler of Sukhothai passed away. Knowing Phra Ruang to be a man of great merit, the citizens joined together and asked him to leave the monkhood to rule the city as King Srichanthrathibodi. After Phra Ruang ascended the throne, Sukhothai flourished and prospered for a thousand years until the time of its eventual collapse.

เมื่อทหารขอมนายหนึ่งพบเบาะแสของพระร่วงจึงไปรายงานเจ้าเมือง
ขอมและอาสาไปฆ่าพระร่วงเอง ทหารขอมนายนั้นเก่งคาถาอาคมมากมี
ฤทธิ์ดำดินได้ จึงใช้ฤทธิ์ดำดินลอดกำแพงเมืองแล้วไปโผล่ที่วัดที่พระร่วง
จำวัดอยู่ ทหารเห็นพระร่วงกำลังกวาดลานวัดอยู่ แต่ไม่รู้จักจึงถามว่า
"พระร่วงที่มาจากเมืองละโว้อยู่ที่ไหน" พระร่วงรู้ตัวทันทีว่ากำลังตกอยู่ใน
อันตราย จึงพูดกับทหารว่า "เจ้าจงอยู่ที่นี่แหละอย่าไปไหนเลย ฉันจะไป
ตามพระร่วงให้" ด้วยฤทธิ์วาจาสิทธิ์ของพระร่วง ร่างของขอมดำดินผู้นั้น
จึงแข็งกลายเป็นหินติดอยู่บนดินตรงนั้นทันที

ต่อมาเมื่อเจ้าเมืองสุโขทัยสวรรคตและชาวเมืองรู้ว่าพระร่วงเป็นผู้มีบุญ
จึงพร้อมใจกันขอให้พระร่วงลาสิกขาบทแล้วอัญเชิญขึ้นเป็นเจ้าเมือง
พระนามว่า พระเจ้าศรีจันทราธิบดี และนับตั้งแต่พระร่วงขึ้นครองราช
สมบัติ กรุงสุโขทัยก็เจริญรุ่งเรือง นับแต่นั้นมานับพันปีจนถึงกาลล่มสลาย

Vocabulary

1	มีชาติกำเนิด	**mii châat gam nèrrt**	to be born into, born as
2	เชื้อสาย	**chúea săay**	lineage
3	พญานาค	**phá yaa nâak**	Phaya Naga (a mythical serpent demigod from Thai folklore)
4	เสนียดจัญไร	**sà-nìat jan-rai**	inauspicious, evil
5	ความอัปมงคล	**khwaam àp-pà mong khon**	misfortune
6	ฟักไข่	**fák khài**	to hatch, incubate
7	วาจาสิทธิ์	**waa jaa sìt**	sacred speech/words
8	ศักดิ์สิทธิ์	**sàk sìt**	sacred
9	พายเรือ	**paay ruea**	to paddle a boat
10	พูดลอย ๆ	**phûut lawy lawy**	to speak absent-mindedly
11	กระแสน้ำ	**grà-săeh náam**	(water/ocean) current
12	ความลับ	**khwaam láp**	secret
13	ส่วย	**sùay**	tribute, tax
14	เกวียน	**gwian**	wagon, cart
15	ไพร่พล, กองทัพ	**phrâi phon, gawng tháp**	soldiers, army
16	บรรทุก, ขน	**ban thúk, khŏn**	to transport, carry
17	เสนอ	**sà-nĕrr**	to propose
18	ภาชนะ	**phaa-chá-ná**	container
19	ชะลอม	**chá lawm**	(bamboo) basket
20	รั่ว	**rûa**	to leak
21	ข้าราชบริพาร	**khâa râat chá baw-rí phaan** (royal word)	courtier, servant of the king
22	พเนจร	**phá-neh jawn**	to wander
23	พระภิกษุ	**phrá phík-sù**	monk

24	เบาะแส	**bàw sǎeh**	clue
25	ดำดิน	**dam din**	to go/dive underground
26	ครองราชสมบัติ	**khrawng râat-chá sǒm-bàt** (royal word)	to ascend the throne

Culture Notes

The myth of Phra Ruang is both a heroic legend based on a real historical person and a fable illustrating the virtue of wisdom. In some historical records, Phra Ruang refers to the first monarch of the Sukhothai Kingdom whose speech was considered magical. Therefore, whenever he spoke or made a decree, it would immediately materialize. For example, as in the story, he is said to have ordered a Khmer spy who had traveled underground to attack him to turn into stone. This is the origin of the Thai expression "**Pak Phra Ruang**," which refers to holy or magical speech that immediately becomes real.

Comprehension Questions

1. พระร่วงรู้ว่าตัวเองมี "วาจาสิทธิ์" เป็นครั้งแรกเมื่ออายุเท่าไร
2. พระร่วงเสนอความคิดกับข้าหลวงให้เปลี่ยนภาชนะใส่น้ำเป็นอะไร
3. ทหารขอมเข้ามาในวัดที่พระร่วงจำวัดได้อย่างไร

Writing Activity

สมมติว่าคุณเป็น "พระร่วง" เขียนจดหมายถึงตัวละครอื่นในนิทานอธิบายเหตุการณ์ที่ทำให้ชีวิตเปลี่ยนหรือได้เรียนรู้ประสบการณ์

Imagine you are Phra Ruang. Write a friendly letter to another character to explain an incident that changed your life or taught you something.

Appendices

A Brief Introduction
to the Thai Language

This book is designed for Thai language learners who have studied reading and writing but lack practice and/or confidence reading Thai, as well as for general readers interested in Thai culture. Below is a brief Introduction to the Thai language including a pronunciation guide and introduction to the writing system. The 28 stories in this book begin short and simple and become longer and more difficult as the book progresses. Each story is accompanied by culture notes, a vocabulary list, some comprehension questions, and a writing activity. These stories are all well-known folk tales that have been passed down from one generation to another and touch on universal human virtues, such as strength and kindness, and events believed to have been shaped by the gods.

Overview of the Thai language

Thai, also known as central Thai, is the official national language of Thailand and is spoken by over 60 million people. It is taught in schools and used in business, the media, and all government affairs throughout the country. The ancient Thai language belongs to the Tai language family of Southeast Asia, which includes languages spoken in Assam, northern Myanmar, Thailand, Laos, northern Vietnam, and the Chinese provinces of Yunnan, Guizhou (Kweichow), and Guangxi (Kwangsi). Outside Bangkok and the central region, there are three other Tai dialects and languages spoken in Thailand: Northern Thai in the north, Southern Thai in the south, and Lao or Northeastern Thai (Isan) in the northeast.

Thai has its own scripts. The oldest example of Thai script that has been found was produced over 1,000 years ago in the Sukhothai period by King Ramkamhaeng. The kingdom of Sukhothai, established in central Thailand in the early to mid-thirteenth century, represents the first major Thai kingdom. In 1283, the Sukhothai Script was created based on the ancient Khmer and Mon scripts, which were in turn derived from southern Indian scripts through the spread of Buddhism and trade contacts in Southeast Asia. These scripts were originally used in the ancient Indian languages of Sanskrit and Pali.

Later, Ayutthaya was established as the capital of Thailand, and "King Narai script" was developed. This has been the official writing system in the country ever since. During Ayutthaya period, a large number of Khmer, Sanskrit, and Pali words were borrowed for use in the Thai language. These loanwords comprise a large portion of the technical vocabulary in science, government, education, religion, and literature.

Basic Thai Grammar

Thai words and sentences are written and read from left to right with no spaces between words. Vowels can appear before, after, above, or below a consonant. In Thai writing, there is no distinction between uppercase and lowercase letters, and the end of a sentence is marked by a space.

Thai grammar is much simpler than those of many European languages. The basic sentence structure in Thai is similar to that in English. Here are some fundamental rules:

- The basic word order is *subject + verb + object* like English.

- No articles like "a," "an," or "the" are used.

- No punctuation is used to indicate a question or the end of a sentence.

- There are no plural forms.

- Thai verbs do not change and have only one simple form regardless of subject or tense. For example, "to eat" is the same whether the subject is I, you, he/she, or they, and whether the action took place in the past, present, or future. So, Thai words never change form.

- Thai has no tense, but you can use the following helping words at the beginning or the end of the sentence to indicate the past or the future:

  1. Time words, such as *now, today, yesterday, tomorrow, six o'clock*, etc. For example:

     Wan-níi chăn mâi sà-baay. Today I'm not feeling well.

     Phrûng níi phŏm wâang. I'm free tomorrow.

  2. Using "láew" แล้ว (already) at the end of the sentence to indicate that something has been completed prior to the moment of speaking. For example,

     Chăn gin yaa láew. I've already taken medicine.

     Phŏm khâo-jai láew. I already understand.

3. Using "jà" จะ (will) in front of a verb to indicate the future sometimes with a time word added to emphasize when it is going to happen in the future. For example,

> **Phrûng-níi khun jà tham à-rai?** What will you do tomorrow?
> **Chăn jà jàay ngerrn-sòt.** I will pay in cash.

- In order to form a question, you add a short question word at the end of the sentence, which is like a verbal question mark.

> **Khun mii phîi náwng mái?** Do you have brothers or sisters?
> **Khun phûut phaa-săa à-rai?** What is your mother tongue?

- For a compound noun that is made up of a **noun** and **adjective**, the structure will be different from that in English. Here are some examples:

> white house = "house + white" = **bâan sĭi khăaw**
> big cat = "cat + big" = **maew yài**

- Thai adjectives can function as verbs without adding any form of the verb "to be" simply by placing the adjective after the noun, as in the following examples:

> Thai food is delicious = Thai food + delicious = **aa-hăan thai + à-ròy**

The following section introduces the Thai writing system. Learning reading and writing can be hard for beginners. You may find it very complicated. But once you get the hang of it, you will probably discover that it is not as hard as you thought.

The Pronunciation of Thai Sounds

Consonants

The 44 consonants are divided into 3 groups: <u>Mid</u>, <u>High</u>, and <u>Low</u>. They are classified by their tonal quality that determines the tone of the syllable.

Mid	High	Low	
ก /g/ **g**un	ข /kh/ **k**ind	ค ฆ /kh/ **k**id	ง /ng/ si**ng**ing
จ /j/ **j**ob	ฉ /ch/ **ch**at	ช ฌ /ch/ **ch**ip	ซ /s/ **s**it
ด ฎ /d/ **d**o	ฐ ฐ /th/ **t**ime	ฑ ฒ ฑ ฒ /th/ **t**oy	
ต ฏ /t/ s**t**op	ผ /ph/ **p**an	พ ภ /ph/ **p**in	น ณ /n/ **n**ew
บ /b/ **b**uy	ฝ /f/ **f**ine	ฟ /f/ **f**un	ม /m/ **m**an
ป /p/ s**p**end	ส ศ ษ /s/ **s**ee	ย ญ /y/ **y**ear	ร /r/ **r**at
อ *a/e/i/o/u **o**ut	ห /h/ **h**ole	ล ฬ /l/ **l**ay	ว /w/ **w**in	ฮ /h/ **h**igh

*Note: The letter "อ" acts as a silent vowel carrier (a/e/i/o/u) at the beginning of words that starts with a vowel.

Consonant Clusters

A consonant cluster is a sequence of two consonants that appear together in the initial position. These can be classified into two types according to their pronunciation.

1. Real clusters.

Real clusters are consonant clusters in which the first and second consonants are pronounced together. There are 15 cluster forms, but only 11 blended phonemes: กร **gr**, กล **gl**, กว **gw**, ปร **pr**, ปล **pl**, ขร/คร **khr**, ขล/คล **khl**, ขว /คว **khw**, พร **phr**, พล/ผล **phl**, and ตร **tr**.

2. False cluster

In false clusters, the first consonant (จ j, ซ s, ส s, ศ s) is pronounced, but the second consonant (ร r) is silent. For example, จริง is pronounced as **jing**.

Final Consonants (Ending)

There are eight final consonants or ending sounds: three "dead" and five "live" endings. Unlike English, all endings are unvoiced.

Stop ending		Live ending	
Form	**Sound**	**Form**	**Sound**
ก	-k "par__k__"	ง	-ng "ha__ng__"
ด	-t "goo__d__"	น	-n "te__n__"
บ	-p "la__b__"	ม	-m "hi__m__"
		ย	-y "bo__y__"
		ว	-w "bo__w__"

Vowels

Single vowels and diphthongs (a combination of two vowels) are generally separated into short and long forms. The terms "long" and "short" refer to the length of time a vowel sound is pronounced.

1. Single vowels

Short			Long		
Form		**Sound**	**Form**		**Sound**
_ั	a	as in ab__ou__t	_า	aa	as in "p__aw__"
_ิ	i	as in h__ea__t (longer)	_ี	ii	as in "fr__ee__"
_ึ	ue	similar to miss__ion__ (mĭshən)	_ื_อ	ueh	as in "fl__ew__" (longer)
_ุ	u	as in b__oo__t	_ู	uu	as in "f__oo__d"
เ_ะ	e	as in g__a__te (shorter)	เ_	eh	as in "p__ay__"
แ_ะ	ae	as in b__a__t (shorter)	แ_	aeh	as in "d__a__m"

Short			Long		
Form		**Sound**	**Form**		**Sound**
ไ_ะ	o	as in "uh-<u>oh</u>!" (shorter)	ไ_	oh	as in "s<u>o</u>"
เ_าะ	aw	as in "h<u>o</u>t"	_อ	aw	as in "<u>or</u>"
เ_อะ	er	as in "bett<u>er</u>" (shorter)	เ_อ	err	as in "p<u>er</u>"
			_ำ	am	as in "b<u>om</u>b"
			ไ_ / ใ_	ai	as in "h<u>ig</u>h"
			เ_า	ao	as in "c<u>ou</u>nt"

2. Diphthongs

Diphthongs are made up of a combination of two single vowels, but pronounced as one syllable.

Form					Sound
เ_ีย	(ii + aa)	=	ia		as in "L<u>ea</u>h"
เ_ือ	(ueh + aa)	=	uea		no similar sound
_ัว	(uu + aa)	=	ua		as in "d<u>o a</u>"

Tones

Thai has five different tones or pitches: *mid, low, falling, high,* and *rising.* Changing the tone of a word will also change its meaning. Tones are written using a tone mark, except neutral mid-level tones, which are not marked.

Tone Mark	Tone Level	Symbol	Example	Meaning
No mark	mid	no mark	ปา **paa**	throw
่	low	` ` ` `	ป่า **pàa**	forest, jungle

Tone Mark	Tone Level	Symbol	Example	Meaning
่	falling	^	ป่า pâa	aunt (mother's older sister)
้	high	´	ป้า páa	an informal term to call one's father derived from Chinese
+	rising	˘	ป๋า păa	an informal term to call one's father derived from Chinese

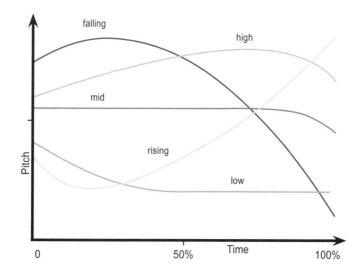

- The mid tone is produced using a constant pitch within your normal vocal range.
- The low tone starts at a pitch lower than your normal vocal range.
- The falling tone starts slightly above your comfortable speaking range and drops below the starting point.
- The high tone rises middle to high, like when asking a question in English.
- The rising tone begins by lowering and then moving upwards.

Reading and Writing:
Thai Vowels and Consonants

1. Vowels

Practice writing the following vowels and saying them out loud.

_ะ	a									
◌ิ	i									
◌ื	ue									
◌ุ	u									
เ_ะ	e									
แ_ะ	ae									
โ_ะ	o									
เ_าะ	aw									
เ_อะ	er									
_า	aa									
◌ี	ii									
◌ือ	ueh									

◌ู	uu									
เ◌	eh									
แ◌	aeh									
โ◌	oh									
◌อ	aw									
เ◌อ	err									
◌ำ	am									
ไ◌	ai									
ใ◌	ai									
เ◌า	ao									
เ◌ีย	ia									
เ◌ือ	uea									
◌ัว	ua									

2. Consonants

Practice writing the consonants in each group and saying them out loud.

2.1 Mid tone consonants

ก	g										
จ	j										
ฎ	d										
ฏ	d										
ต	t										
ฏ	t										
บ	b										
ป	p										
อ	a/e/i/ o/u										

2.2 High tone consonants

ข	kh										
ฉ	ch										
ถ	th										
ฐ	th										

ผ	ph									
ฝ	ph									
ส	s									
ศ	s									
ษ	s									
ห	h									

2.3 Low tone consonants

ค	kh									
ง	ng									
ช	ch									
ฌ	ch									
ซ	s									
ท	th									
ธ	th									
ฑ	th									

ฒ	th										
พ	ph										
ภ	ph										
น	n										
ณ	n										
ฟ	f										
ม	m										
ย	y										
ญ	y										
ร	r										
ล	l										
ฬ	l										
ว	w										
ฮ	h										

3. Tone marks

Practice writing the following tone marks.

่											
๋											
๋											
+											

Reading and Writing: Thai Words and Sentences

Thai writing differs from that of many other languages in that there are no spaces between words.

Each syllable is composed of up to four parts: the initial consonant (C), vowel (V), ending (E), and tone mark (T).

> Initial consonant + Vowel + Ending (optional) + Tone mark (optional)
> (C + V + E + T)

1. Initial consonant + Vowel

C	+	V		C	+	V	
ก	+	-ะ	กะ	ฝ	+	-า	ฝา
จ	+	◌ิ	จิ	ป	+	◌ี	ปี
ข	+	เ◌	เข	ห	+	แ◌	แห
ด	+	◌ุ	ดุ	ฟ	+	◌ู	ฟู
ง	+	เ◌าะ	เงาะ	บ	+	เ◌า	เบา
น	+	เ◌อะ	เนอะ	ธ	+	เ◌อ	เธอ
ส	+	เ◌ีย	เสีย	ร	+	เ◌ือ	เรือ

Practice: Combine the consonants and vowels below to form syllables. The first one has already been completed as an example.

C + V	ต + เ◌า	ช + -อ	ผ + เ◌อ	ย + ◌ึ-า	ท + ◌ี◌	ว + แ-ะ
Syllable	เตา					
C + V	พ + ◌ู	ส + ไ-	ม + ◌ี◌	ต + โ-	ฮ + เ◌ีย	บ + ◌ัว
Syllable						

2. Initial consonant + Vowel + Ending (Final Consonants)

C	V	E	Syllable
จ	-า	ก	= จาก
พ	◌ุ	ด	= พูด
ร	◌ี	บ	= รีบ
ย	แ-	น	= แยน
ป	โ-	ง	= โปง

Practice: Combine consonants, vowels, and endings to form syllables. The first one has already been completed as an example.

C + V + E	บ + เ- + น	ส + -อ + บ	ป + เ◌ีย + ก	ย + ◌ุ + ง
Syllable	เบน			
C + V + E	ค + ◌ี + น	ฝ + แ- + ด	ด + เ-อ + ย	จ + ◌ี + น
Syllable				

3. Tone Mark Position

- In syllables without a double consonant (two consonants next to each other), tone marks are always placed above the initial consonant.

  Examples: ได้ บ้าน อ่าน

- If the consonant has a superscript vowel, the tone mark is placed above that vowel.

  Examples: ชื่อ พี่ เสื้อ

- In cases in which there is a double consonant, the tone mark is placed above the second consonant.

  Examples: อร่อย หน้า สร้าง

4. Tone rules

Tones are an essential part of Thai language, as using the wrong tone can completely change the meaning of a word. In order to accurately differentiate among tones, it is important to learn about tone-related rules and the tonal composition of Thai syllables.

The tone of a syllable is determined by a combination of the following factors:

- Initial consonant (mid, high, or low)
- Vowel (short or long)
- Final consonant (stop ending or live ending)
- Tone marks (if any)

4.1 Mid consonants + vowels + endings + tone marks

Mid Consonants	Vowels		Endings				Tone marks			
	Long (L.V.)	Short (S.V.)	Stop ก ด บ (L.V.)	(S.V.)	Live น ง ม ย ว (L.V.)	(S.V.)	่	้	๊	+
ก จ ด ต บ ป ฎ ฏ	→ กา gaa	↓ กะ gà	↓ กาก gàak	↓ กัด gàt	→ กาน gaan	→ กัน gan	↓ ก่า gàa	∩ ก้า gâa	╱ ก๊า gáa	∪ ก๋า gǎa

Practice reading the following words.

→	↓	∩	╱	∪
	จิ		จิ๊	
	ปุ		ปุ๊	
ปี	ปี่	ปี้	ปี๊	ปี๋
ตือ	ตื่อ	ตื้อ	ตื๊อ	ตื๋อ
ดู	ดู่	ดู้	ดู๊	ดู๋
บาน	บ่าน	บ้าน	บ๊าน	บ๋าน
แตง	แต่ง	แต้ง	แต๊ง	แต๋ง
	กุด		กุ๊ด	

4.2 High consonants + vowels + endings + tone marks

High Consonants	Vowels		Endings				Tone marks			
	Long (L.V.)	Short (S.V.)	Stop ก ด บ (L.V.)	(S.V.)	Live น ง ม ย ว (L.V.)	(S.V.)	่	้	๊	+
ข ฉ ถ ฐ ผ ฝ ส ศ ษ ห	↶ ขา khǎa	↓ เขะ khè	↓ ขาด khàat	↓ ขัด khàt	↶ ขาน khǎan	↶ ขัน khan	↓ ข่า khàa	⌃ ข้า khâa		

Practice reading the following words:

↶	↓	⌃
	เถาะ	
	เหอะ	
แฉ	แฉ่	แฉ้
โถ	โถ่	โถ้
หอ	ห่อ	ห้อ
เผอ	เผ่อ	เผ้อ
สาย	ส่าย	ส้าย
ขึ้น	ขึ่น	ขึ้น
	ผูก	

4.3 Low consonants + vowels + endings + tone marks

Low Consonants	Vowels		Endings				Tone marks			
	Long (L.V.)	Short (S.V.)	Stop ก ด บ (L.V.)	(S.V.)	Live น ง ม ย ว (L.V.)	(S.V.)	่	้	๊	+
ค ง ช ฌ ท ธ ฑ ฒ ร น ณ ม ว ย ญ ล ฟ	→ มา maa	↗ มะ má	⌃ มาก mâak	↗ มัด mát	→ แมน maehn	→ มัน man	⌃ ม่า mâa	↗ ม้า máa		

Practice reading the following words:

→	∩	↗
	ค่ะ	คะ
	ล่ะ	ละ
คู	คู่	คู้
โง	โง่	โง้
ชือ	ชื่อ	ชื้อ
พอ	พ่อ	พ้อ
ฟา	ฟ้า	ฟ้า
นิม	นิ่ม	นิ้ม
	เลือก	
		ยุบ

Practice: Identify the tones and read aloud. The first one has already been completed as an example.

บ้าน	เขียน	ห้อง	โดด	โน่น	ทุ่ม	ซ้าย	เพื่อน	เต้น	ร้อง	ก๊วน	คืน	ก๋วย	เตี๋ยว
∩													

Practice reading writing the following words:

I, me (female speaker)	**chăn**	ฉัน	
I, me (male speaker)	**phŏm**	ผม	
name	**chûeh**	ชื่อ	
nickname	**chûeh-lên**	ชื่อเล่น	
last name	**naam-sà-gun**	นามสกุล	
come from	**maa-jàak**	มาจาก	

country	**prà-thêt**	ประเทศ	
Thank you.	**khàwp-khun**	ขอบคุณ	
Excuse me./ I am sorry.	**khǎw-thôht**	ขอโทษ	
You're welcome./ That's all right.	**mâi-pen-rai**	ไม่เป็นไร	
eat	**gin**	กิน	
like	**châwp**	ชอบ	
dislike	**mâi- châwp**	ไม่ ชอบ	
hungry	**hǐw**	หิว	
not hungry	**mâi- hǐw**	ไม่ หิว	
delicious, yummy	**à-ròi**	อร่อย	
not delicious, not yummy	**mâi-à-ròi**	ไม่ อร่อย	
I'd like…. / May I have….?	**khǎw…**	ขอ……	

Practice reading and writing the following phrase and sentences:

My name is….	**chǎn chûe / phǒm chûe**	ฉัน ชื่อ…/ผม ชื่อ	
I am from ….	**chǎn/phǒm maa-jàak prà-thêt**	ฉัน/ผม มาจาก ประเทศ	
How are you?	**sà-baay-dii mái**	สบายดีไหม	
I am fine.	**sà-baay-dii**	สบายดี	
I don't understand.	**mâi-khâo-jai**	ไม่เข้าใจ	
I don't know.	**mâi-rúu**	ไม่รู้	

Speak slowly, please.	phôut cháa-cháa	พูดช้าๆ	
I am feeling sick.	chăn/phŏm mâi sà-baay	ฉัน/ผม ไม่ สบาย	
I am allergic to...	chăn/phŏm pháeh...	ฉัน/ผม แพ้.......	
I am tired.	chăn/phŏm nùeay	ฉัน/ผม เหนื่อย	
I am lost.	chăn/phŏm lŏng-thaang	ฉัน/ผม หลงทาง	
I am a vegetarian.	chăn/phŏm gin jay	ฉัน/ผม กินเจ	
I am hungry.	chăn/phŏm hĭw	ฉัน/ผม หิว	
I am thirsty.	chăn/phŏm hĭw náam	ฉัน/ผม หิวน้ำ	
I am already full.	chăn/phŏm ìm láehw	ฉัน/ผม อิ่มแล้ว	
Where is the bathroom?	hâwng-nám yòu thîi-năi	ห้องน้ำอยู่ที่ไหน	
How much is it?	thâo-rài	เท่าไร	
Can you lower the price?	lót dâi-mái	ลดได้ไหม	
Can you help me?	chûay chăn/phŏm dâi-mái	ช่วย ฉัน/ผม ได้ไหม	
What time is it?	gìi-mong	กี่โมง	
Can you speak English?	khun phûut phaa-săa-ang-grìt dâi-mái	คุณพูดภาษาอังกฤษได้ไหม	

How do you say this in Thai?	phaa-săa-thai phûut yang-ngai	ภาษาไทยพูดยัง ไง	

Practice writing the following sentences in Thai script.

1. khun châwp gin à-rai (What do you like to eat?)

_____

2. weh-laa-wâang phŏm châwp lên-don-trii láew-kâw râwng-phleng kráp
   (In my free time, I like playing musical instruments and also singing.)

_____

3. chăn rúu-sùek wian-hŭa (I'm feeling dizzy.)

_____

4. khăw thîi-nâng rim nâa-tàang (Can I get a window seat?)

_____

5. ráp bàt-khreh-dìt mái (Do you accept credit cards?)

_____

Audio Tracklist

How to access the audio recordings for this book:

1. Check to be sure you have an Internet connection.
2. Type the URL below into to your web browser.

https://www.tuttlepublishing.com/thai-stories-for-language-learners

For support you can email us at info@tuttlepublishing.com.

"Books to Span the East and West"

Tuttle Publishing was founded in 1832 in the small New England town of Rutland, Vermont [USA]. Our core values remain as strong today as they were then—to publish best-in-class books which bring people together one page at a time. In 1948, we established a publishing office in Japan—and Tuttle is now a leader in publishing English-language books about the arts, languages and cultures of Asia. The world has become a much smaller place today and Asia's economic and cultural influence has grown. Yet the need for meaningful dialogue and information about this diverse region has never been greater. Over the past seven decades, Tuttle has published thousands of books on subjects ranging from martial arts and paper crafts to language learning and literature—and our talented authors, illustrators, designers and photographers have won many prestigious awards. We welcome you to explore the wealth of information available on Asia at **www.tuttlepublishing.com**.

Published by Tuttle Publishing, an imprint of Periplus Editions (HK) Ltd.

www.tuttlepublishing.com

Copyright © 2022 by Periplus Editions (HK) Ltd.

Cover image © Kwanchai | Shutterstock

Library of Congress Control Number: 2022935227

ISBN 978-0-8048-5378-1

First edition
25 24 23 22   6 5 4 3 2 1   2204TP

Printed in Singapore

Distributed by

North America, Latin America & Europe
Tuttle Publishing, 364 Innovation Drive
North Clarendon, VT 05759-9436 U.S.A.
Tel: 1 (802) 773-8930 Fax: 1 (802) 773-6993
info@tuttlepublishing.com
www.tuttlepublishing.com

Japan
Tuttle Publishing, Yaekari Building 3rd Floor
5-4-12 Osaki Shinagawa-ku, Tokyo 141 0032
Tel: (81) 3 5437-0171 Fax: (81) 3 5437-0755
sales@tuttle.co.jp
www.tuttle.co.jp

Asia Pacific
Berkeley Books Pte. Ltd.
3 Kallang Sector #04-01, Singapore 349278
Tel: (65) 6741-2178 Fax: (65) 6741-2179
inquiries@periplus.com.sg
www.tuttlepublishing.com

TUTTLE PUBLISHING® is a registered trademark of Tuttle Publishing, a division of Periplus Editions (HK) Ltd.